LITTLE IMBER ON THE DOWN

Little Imber on the Down

Salisbury Plain's Ghost Village

REX SAWYER

First published in the United Kingdom in 2001 by
The Hobnob Press, PO Box 1838, East Knoyle, Salisbury SP3 6FA

Reprinted with minor corrections 2003

First published in paperback 2008, reprinted with minor changes 2010

British Library Cataloguing in Publication Data
A catalogue record for this book is available from the British Library.

ISBN (paperback edition) 978-1-906978-24-2

Typeset in 11/15 pt Souvenir Light
Typesetting and origination by John Chandler
Printed in Great Britain by Lightning Source

Contents

DEDICATION

To the People of Imber
To Betty Hooper who chronicled its story
To Austin Underwood who championed its cause

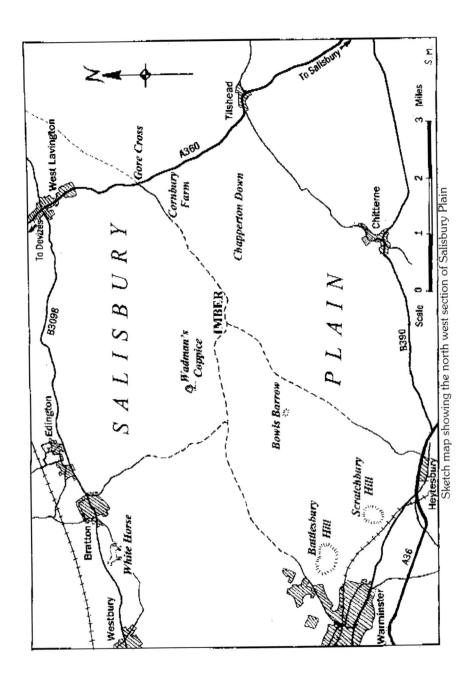

Sketch map showing the north west section of Salisbury Plain

Introduction

In a hatbox full of Imber resources at Devizes Museum, among the faded photographs, yellowing newspaper cuttings and other assorted memorabilia, I came across a school exercise book. It contained a project on the story of Imber and commenced with the words, 'Can so small a place have a history?' The anonymous reply on the next line, uttered with simple country logic, is difficult to dispute: 'Folk have lived about there for 3,000 years so something must have happened.'

In fact one could be forgiven for thinking otherwise. Its very isolation among the moist hills of Salisbury Plain protected Imber from many of the historic disturbances sweeping the country over the centuries. There is no evidence of religious or civil disturbance, no rick burning or annihilation by plague. No village rogue was condemned to the gallows nor saintly cleric canonised. As Mrs Molly Archer-Smith is fond of reminding me, until the Second World War and the enforced removal of the entire population, few from Imber had visited the cinema or even seen a train!

It is perhaps true to say that Imber folk were content with their daily round and annual agricultural cycle, shielded by the anonymity wrought by such isolation, but it is sad that the one historic 'happening' that led to their appearance on the national stage should have been the demise of their village. On 1 November 1943, the inhabitants were informed by the War Office that they had six weeks to prepare for evacuation. Their village, situated in the middle of the Imber ranges to the north of Salisbury Plain, was required to help prepare the American army for the imminent invasion of Europe. With reluctant acceptance of the situation, fuelled by patriotism, the villagers made their arrangements to leave fully convinced that they would return to their homes when the war ended. That was not to be.

There were, of course, other villages where residents suffered the same distressing fate. The parishioners of Tyneham and East Holme along the beautiful Dorset coastal ridgeway were similarly evicted. Tottington moulders within the MOD's Stanford training area in southern Norfolk. Nearer to home, not so many miles north of Imber, lay the tiny community of Snap, some fifteen houses contained within 413 acres of land. Rural decay was already evident when it was used as a training ground and machine gun ranges during the First World War. The occasional mound ringed by barbed wire is all that remains now. On Salisbury Plain many farms and properties were closed down for the duration of the Second World War but only at Imber were the inhabitants unable to return when hostilities ceased.

Would Imber have survived had the army not stepped in to settle the matter? Statistics would indicate it is unlikely. From a high point of 440 souls in 1851, the censuses show a steady decline to 152 in 1931, the last such exercise to be carried out within the village. There is some disagreement about the number remaining in November 1943. Figures of between 100 and 150 have been quoted; Army statistics quote 135. Certainly many younger members of the community were happy to find themselves living in areas of greater social activity. Nevertheless, circumstances have changed considerably since the war, particularly with greater mobility and the continuing development of mechanisation. Local farmers like Sydney Dean were always keen to return and cultivate their fertile acres. There is also an increasing demand from town and city dwellers to live within more remote rural settings. As one resigned ex-villager put it, 'If it had survived, it wouldn't be what it was. It would have turned into a yuppie village!'

Speculation along these lines, however, is academic. The army appears to require its ranges on the Plain more than at any time since 1945. I can think of no period when the Imber area has been open to the public anything like the maximum 50 days a year recommended by the 1961 Public Inquiry.

The story of Imber has been told and re-told on numerous occasions in newspapers, magazines and, more recently, in television documentaries. The time is ripe, nearly 60 years after the evacuation, for a re-evaluation, and I am grateful to the media who have kept Imber alive in people's minds. I have tried to use their record of events and enable the people who were involved - the villagers, the military, the politicians and other observers - to speak for themselves. Over the course of time history and mythology can become inextricably mixed and I have tried to use the most reliable sources I could find. In the well-documented story of Matthew Dean's robbery, for example, I referred to several of the accounts given at the time.

There are so many who have given generously of their time and resources to piece together the events. My journeys and correspondence took me into many places, even Scotland, to locate them. In particular I must express my grateful thanks to the late Betty Hooper whose record of Imber in photographs and reminiscences is unsurpassed. Her assistance with this book and the earlier ones I researched with Peter Daniels for *Salisbury Plain; the Archive Photographs Series* was enthusiastic and instructive. Since her death I have received the same generous access and assistance with proof reading from her children, Rosalind and Richard. For this I am deeply grateful. Mary Underwood, widow of Austin, has given me unfailing encouragement and access to her husband's photographic legacy of the events with which he was associated. Terry Crawford (author of *Wiltshire and the Great War*) has assisted me enormously with his own resources and much helpful advice along the way. I am also grateful to Mollie Archer-Smith and Suzette Gordon-Johnson for the use of their photographic material and details of the Dean family. Jean Morrison from Bratton was, as ever, open-handed in her contribution of stories and resources from Imber's past. Among the (sadly) few remaining residents of Imber and other close relatives I should like to acknowledge my thanks to Audrey Streeting, Derrick Mitchell, Jack Yeates, Gwen Gentry, Ellis Daniels, Michael Daniels, Ken Cruse and Reg Meaden. Others whose input I have valued were Peter Daniels, Norman Parker, Sheila Nankiwell, Christine Richardson, Catherine Targett, Sophie Annetts, David Marshall, Richard Shellabear, Richard Pierce, and Stephen Moody who produced the sketch maps.

Among the various institutions who so willingly assisted me and to whom I should like to record my appreciation were Salisbury Local History and Reference Library (always my first port of call), the Public Record Office at Kew, the Wiltshire and Swindon Record Office at Trowbridge, the Salisbury

& South Wiltshire Museum, the Wiltshire Archaeological and Natural History Society Library and Museum, Devizes, and Warminster Library. I should like to acknowledge the advice and assistance of my friend Dr John Chandler, of Lt Col (retd) Nigel de Foubert who read my manuscript from the military point of view and made helpful suggestions, and Ian Barnes, Senior Environmental Advisor for the Plain for his help with the archaeological content. As ever, my final thanks must go to my wife, Sheila, for her encouragement and help with the script.

REX SAWYER
Tisbury, June 2001

REX SAWYER was headmaster of Wilton Secondary and Middle Schools for eighteen years. He was also a counsellor for the Open University, a lecturer for the WEA, and a Salisbury magistrate. He has written a number of books and articles on South Wiltshire and Salisbury Plain, and lives at Tisbury.

Previous Publications

Care and the Community (collab. John White), Ginns 1971
The Bowerchalke Parish Papers, Alan Sutton 1989
The Nadder Valley in Old Photographs, Alan Sutton 1994
Tales of a Wiltshire Valley: The Nadder, Alan Sutton 1995
Salisbury Plain: the Archives Photographs (collab. Peter Daniels), Chalford 1996
Salisbury Plain: a Second Selection (collab. Peter Daniels), Chalford 1997
Highway Patrol (children's novel), Abacus 1998
South Wiltshire: Images of England (collab. Peter Daniels), Chalford 1999

1 From the Earliest of Days

Little Imber on the Downe
Seven miles from any towne.
Ship bleats the unly sounds.
Life twer sweet, with ne'er a vrown,
Oh let us bide on Imber Downe.

Imber has been deserted now (in 2001) for 58 years, its once pleasant cottages and well-tended gardens reduced to a wasteland of shattered remnants. The wind blows cheerlessly through gaping doorways and windows now long invaded by creeping vegetation. Yet this was once a close knit community, frequently cut off in winter, its independence forged by its isolation among the chalk hills of Salisbury Plain. Lying in a secluded wooded valley at the foot of Rough Down, its soil trodden only by soldiers, its silence disturbed by the song of larks and the sound of distant guns, it has completed a long and honourable life cycle brought to an untimely end.

It is not known with any certainty when the original settlement, which became known as Imber, was established. The village lies deep in the weathered downland to the north-west of the Plain bordered to the west by the magnificent escarpments of Scratchbury and Battlesbury, and the market town of Warminster. In prehistoric times, Salisbury Plain was the meeting place of many routes, some covering long distances and still surviving as footpaths and byways. The existence of ancient trackways in the Imber area would indicate that economic activity took place there from a very early period. Darbyshire's map of the Green Roads, for example, shows the western branch of the Ridgeway from Urchfont towards Warminster passing through Imber. A further road from Trowbridge passes through Bratton Castle and intersects with a track from Heytesbury near Bowls Barrow to the south before reaching Imber. In 1675 John Ogilby recorded a prominent downland track also adjacent to Bowls Barrow which was part of an ancient route from Westbury to Amesbury.

Further evidence of prehistoric activity is shown by the existence of barrows. As with Salisbury Plain as a whole, this isolated western district is rich in archeological detail. Neolithic long barrows sit on the heights while the later Bronze Age round barrows spread more generally across the landscape, often congregating around water courses. Field systems are found over the majority of the Plain, and they are especially prevalent around the Imber area.

Bowls Barrow is the most prominent long barrow. Estimated to be about 4,500 years old, this ancient monument is believed to incorporate in its structure a massive bluestone weighing about five hundredweight and identical to the bluestones of Stonehenge. It has been conjectured that the stone was removed by a Neolithic chieftain from the supply going by river to Stonehenge for the construction of the bluestone circle, possibly for some ritualistic or healing purpose. However, the facts remain unclear and there is some doubt over the records, leaving scope for further investigation. While excavating there in 1801, the archaeologist William Cunnington found fourteen human skulls lying on a bed of flints and sarsen stones with the skulls of oxen lying on top of the deposit. Further exploration had to be abandoned when heavy stones from the overhanging bank rolled down on to his labourers making the work too dangerous.

During the winter of 1916, an extensive series of military trenches was dug on the down above and to the west of Imber. Fifteen skeletons were discovered, mostly in wooden coffins, their large clenched iron nails still lying in the cavities. Unfortunately, the human remains were removed at an early stage, but the site is believed to have been of Romano-British origin, a theory reinforced by the discovery of small brass coins depicting Constantine and other Roman emperors, found in the Imber area. A settlement of this period, excavated by Sir Richard Colt Hoare, lies near Wadman's Coppice on the ridge above Imber. There is also an exceptional Romano-British settlement at Chapperton Down some 3 km to the east. Much damage would have taken place in the past through military exercises but, since the 1961 Public Inquiry, the marking of the most important sites, and the re-routing of some existing tracks to divert tank activities, has helped to protect these more sensitive historical areas.

Although the origins of the tiny settlement at Imber are obscure, the physical evidence seems to show, therefore, that it evolved, possibly as a Romano-British settlement like those at Wadman's Coppice and Chapperton Down, long before the Norman Conquest. It was certainly well established by the Saxon period and was probably part of the Abbess of Romsey's Edington estate which was established and endowed with land around 967 AD. In 1086 it was recorded in the Domesday Book: 'Radulfus himself holds *Imemerie*'. But the tax was merely for two hides (perhaps approximating to 240 acres) and represented only that portion of the village held by Radulfus. There were two plough teams, a cottager and four bordars, men of the lowest rank in feudal society. There were also three furlongs of pasture. The rest, and much larger portion, would have been taxed under the Abbess's Edington estate. Radulfus was Ralph Mortimer, one of William the Conqueror's Norman warlords. He was created Earl of Hereford and built Wigmore Castle there. Because of this connection, Imber was described for many years as part of 'The Honour of Wigmore.'

The name *Imemerie* in the Domesday Book, and *Immere* in later documents (among other variants) probably indicates a boundary, or mere of Imma. This may well be borne out by the fact that the village originally consisted of two parts lying north and south of the road and the troublesome watercourse known as Imber Dock which runs through the village. Certainly the boundary line of the old hundreds of Heytesbury and Rowborough (later part of Swanborough) runs through the parish at this point. The population was then about 50, probably with the Abbess's estate lying south of the village street near the church, with a smaller settlement to the north. The insignificance of this tiny community may be reckoned by a rental of 1282 when part of the manor was granted to Robert de Immerew and Joan his wife for a yearly rendering of 'one clove gillyflower'!

Evidence of Imber in these relatively lawless times is largely incidental. In 1293 John the Smith of Imer gave evidence against John le Bakere of Puddletown saying that he came into his pasture on the Friday before Whitsun and stole his mare. On Tuesday after Midsummer the smith recognised his horse in the new city of Salisbury. The defendant said he bought the mare at Lopene Fair [Lopen near Crewkerne] in Somerset and was able to bring witnesses as to his character. This led to an acquittal. Among the prisoners held in appalling conditions at Old Salisbury Castle in 1304 were John de Scherston and Adam Attewel 'for slaying Gilbert Sidemounte of Imere in Heghbyr' field'. The castle, at Old Sarum, had been converted into a prison in the mid-13th century and by this time was near the point of collapse. In the same prison was Gilbert Henry, a native of Imber, charged with another man for the murder of his neighbour Walter Seld, but there are no details of the trial or sentence.

Its very isolation on the Plain may have protected Imber from the ravages of the Black Death in 1348 so evident in the surrounding, more populous, areas. Other towns and villages declined significantly in the post-plague era whereas by 1377 Imber's population had risen to 250. Part of the village had been granted by Henry II to his chamberlain John de Rous and soon afterwards much of the Abbess's land was leased by the same family in perpetuity, for an annual rent of £10. Although the family appears to have resided there, little is known of them apart from two stone effigies previously in St Giles's Church, and now, like so many of its possessions, in Edington Priory. Walter, First Lord Hungerford, whose arms appear above the church porch, was the next possessor of the manor. Following his death in 1459, his wife Margaret endowed the Hungerford Chapel at Salisbury Cathedral in her husband's memory. This chantry was dissolved in 1545, but a hundred years later it is recorded that '£22 18s.5d. was paid annually from Imber in two equal parts: at the great western door of the cathedral on the day of the Annunciation of the Blessed Virgin, and on that of St Michael'.

Following the Dissolution much of the previously church-owned land was granted to Sir Thomas Seymour (who later married Henry VIII's widow) and then to the Thynnes at Longleat. Later prominent families associated with the village included the Gawens in the 17th century and the Wadmans from Tinhead Court, who rebuilt Imber Court on the site of an earlier manor house and left generous provision for the future needs of the poor. There was even a Wadman ghost, a lady of the house who appeared intermittently in the attic with a lighted candle!

St Giles Church, Imber, in 1807, from a watercolour painting by John Buckler. The Norman church was rebuilt in 1280. A century later the tower and north porch were added and the wagon roof constructed.

Imber remained through the ensuing centuries a tiny upland village, its roads little more than tracks, lying within the rolling downland of the austere north of the Plain. Its neighbours, well out of view, would have provided little assistance in times of need. Nearest were Edington and Bratton below the steep escarpment which forms the northern edge of the Plain, and the little villages of the Till – Tilshead, Shrewton and Winterbourne Stoke – well to the east. Chitterne, another isolated community, lay to the south and the developing town of Warminster to the west. The familiar rhyme, passed down with many variations, would appear very apt: *'Little Imber on the Down | Seven miles from any town.'*

Such isolation produced a tightly-knit and independent community, but the brooding presence of the surrounding hills within which the village lay must have brought periods of great loneliness to many. Only the ancient tracks, measured by chalk piles to guide the wandering stranger or the farmer back from market, would have provided links with the outside world.

The five-pinnacled church of St Giles was a comforting sight to returning travellers as they crested the down. This 13th-century church and its Norman predecessor would have been a bastion of the village in time of flood, fire and pestilence. Situated south of the village and now divested of its previous interior furnishings, it still provides traces of a fine mural on the north wall. This consists of a collection of animals and human figures worked in brown paint re-discovered during restoration work in 1849.

The Norman font from St Giles Church now at Brixton Deverill.

Edgar Glanfield, who was vicar of Imber from 1917-24, tells us that the fresco relates the story of the patron saint of the church, St Giles, who lived as a hermit near Nîmes in France. One day Flavius Wamba, king of the Goths, came upon his cell while out hunting. Although a violent warlike man, the king was deeply impressed by St Giles's sincerity and calm and was converted to Christianity. Flavius Wamba founded a monastery near the spot for St Giles in 673 AD. The cult of St Giles spread, partly through returning crusaders to other parts of Europe. In England 162 ancient churches were dedicated to him including that at Imber. Faint traces of other decorations, so much a feature of earlier times, can also be found in the dimly-lit south aisle.

One incident of less than neighbourly love within St Giles's Church is recorded in the Wiltshire Quarter Sessions Rolls of 1646. Elizabeth Courtlie complained that during the Sunday service she was abused by Mary Gibbes, 'who with a pin thrust her, the said Elizabeth, in the bodie and with her hands and fingers pinched her and at the same time called her whore and bid her goe to Mr Olives and steal victuals'. In her defence Mary Gibbes protested that she had been pulled by the arm in a violent manner by Elizabeth Courtlie who had pinched her and trodden upon her in the pew. There is no report of the outcome of this incident although the scandalised congregation doubtless had plenty to say!

From the tower of St Giles you become aware of the vulnerability of Imber. It is set in a valley through which Imber Dock gathered up the local springs in stormy weather. Richard Colt Hoare, in his *History of Modern Wiltshire* (1822), describes the cycle of flood and drought:

> The downs which surround this village afford excellent pasture for large flocks of sheep. The air is remarkably pure, and the chief inconvenience seems to arise from an irregularity in the supply of water. At one season the springs, bursting as it were from every pore, form quite a river; while at another they are from 80 to 90 feet below the surface.

The tiny cottages with whitewashed mud walls would have provided little protection at such times. And floods there were in abundance, washing down from the hills on the Warminster side and bursting the banks of the winterbourne with devilish unpredictability on their way to cause further havoc at Chitterne. The water-table was then much higher than it is now, with a consequent effect on the amount of water flowing through the village. It was Imber Dock which brought the village out of its accustomed anonymity in Charles II's reign when Thomas Chambers was indicted at the Quarter Sessions for diverting the course of the stream and causing, it was said, the village street to flood.

It appears that the prosecution arose entirely through the jealousy of two of the more wealthy inhabitants. According to the prosecution:

Thomas Chambers diverted a certain common watercourse in the close there called Ye Home Close, on to the king's high road there leading from Warminster . . . at the lower end of the street in Imber aforesaid, whereby the King's high road is flooded and damaged to the common nuisance and heavy damage of all the lieges and subjects of our said Lord the King passing and travelling in, through, and across the aforesaid road.

In defence Mr Chamber's counsel explained to the court that forty years previously the land in question on the west side of the high street and adjacent to the brook had belonged to a Mr Ayliffe. At that time, due to the action of flooding 'caused upon violent raynes or suddoyne thawes' the unmetalled road had broken up and become dangerous to travellers. The villagers had therefore approached Mr Ayliffe and entreated him to allow a new section of highway to be made on his land. One of the many witnesses speaking on Mr Chamber's behalf said that, 'the old way was so miry that one plough could scarce draw out another'.

Ten years later, Mr Ayliffe had sold his land to a Dr Davenaunant who confirmed this account and said that Mr Ayliffe had even dug two large trenches to further protect the highway and to water his meadow. This apparently had caused envy among certain landowners, including Mr Harris and Mr Polden who had brought the charge. They had also tried to intimidate the poorer villagers – who might later require poor relief – into withholding their evidence.

Unfortunately, we are not told of the outcome of this trial, but the parish records continued to give dire accounts of misery brought to the inhabitants by the intrusion of floods. In 1757, for example, water came from the direction of Broken Cross, Ladywell and Southdown House into Imber. The walls of the mud-built cottages were undermined, several buildings collapsed and it is alleged that several villagers perished. On 19 January 1764, 'The Springs come from Broken Cross and fromme Ladyes Well and South Down into Imber'. On 20 September 1768, 'the Springs broke and was very high'. Deep snow was reported in 1773 and in the following March worse was to come: 'The Springs were higher than ever was known in the memory of man'. Two cottages were swept away and completely destroyed in that disastrous flood. An inquest in January 1791 tells the sad, but probably not exceptional, story of Betty Grant, who, 'in going over the down from

Lavington to Imber in wet and tempestuous weather and being bewildered there fell to the ground and died'.

Nor were the vagaries of the weather the only cause for concern. Nearly all the cottages, farmhouses and outbuildings were thatched. If one caught fire it would send sparks flying and therefore set light to others. One particularly bad fire on 10 June 1770 must have affected the village sorely. Response to an appeal, recorded as far away as Longburton in Dorset, was generous and the funds were still being distributed to the unfortunate inhabitants three years later, as an announcement in the *Salisbury and Winchester Journal* relates:

> Notice is hereby given, that the Trustees named in the brief for the sufferers by fire at Imber, are desired to meet at the house of Thomas Wort, being the Bell inn there, on Tuesday the 9th of Nov, inst at eleven o'clock in the forenoon, in order to make a further distribution of the money collected under the said brief, and that all persons who claim the benefit of the same, are desired to attend at the same time and place.

The vast open stretches of the Plain, its troughs and wooded hollows, the absence of roads, all gave opportunity for robbery and violence. Ella Noyes wrote about Salisbury Plain in 1913:

> The fear of robbers on the Plain was well founded. Camden, writing in the 16th century, says that the district had 'in late times, a bad name for robberies here committed'. The long distance between the inhabited places, the want of roads – the ways being mere tracks in the turf, easily missed by the inexperienced traveller – the opportunities of speed for a good horse upon the open downs, all gave great advantage to the highwayman.
>
> In the 17th and 18th centuries, the Plain was much frequented by some notable gentlemen of that profession. During bad times of unemployment and distress among the poor, men made desperate by need would commit deeds of violence upon solitary travellers on the downs. Even up to about 70 years [c.1840] farmers from the isolated villages never went to market without being well armed.

Travellers through the bleak northern reaches of the Plain, among them farmers attending the markets at Warminster and Devizes, were particularly

A postcard showing the Robbers' Stone on Chitterne Down. A similar stone is situated at Gore's Cross along the Salisbury–Devizes road where the attack on Matthew Dean took place on 21 October 1839.

vulnerable to footpads and highwaymen. The parish records at Imber record the deaths of two brigands, Grimes and Baldwin, in 1716. Having robbed several persons on their return from the Saturday market at Warminster, they became separated. Grimes was apprehended and shot by Edward Slade of Chitterne near Warminster Furze. He was brought dead into Imber and buried in the churchyard on the following day. His accomplice was shot on West Lavington Down. Still alive but seriously wounded, Baldwin was brought to the village of West Lavington where he died and was buried the following day. Grimes was a recurrent offender recognised locally by the scar on his cheek and the confession given by Baldwin before his death.

The most celebrated instance of highway robbery involving Imber occurred in the following century and gives an early introduction to the two most prominent farming families, the Deans and the Hoopers, connected with the community right up to the evacuation. Although accounts differ in detail, the stark facts are recorded on a plain rectangular stone at Gore Cross along the main Devizes to Salisbury road:

> At this spot Mr Dean of Imber was attacked and robbed by four highwaymen in the evening of October 21, 1839. After a spirited pursuit of three hours, one of the felons, Benjamin Colclough, fell dead on Chitterne down. Thomas Saunders, George Waters and Richard Harris were eventually captured and were convicted at the ensuing quarter sessions at Devizes and transported for the term of 15 years. This monument is erected by public subscription as a warning to those who presumptuously think to escape the punishment God has threatened against thieves and robbers.

These were desperate times for farm workers. Agricultural depression, the new poor law removing outdoor relief, soldiers returning from the Napoleonic Wars flooding the market, the mechanisation of farms, all depressed wages and caused widespread unemployment. There is no evidence of rick-burning or machine-breaking at Imber but bands of disenchanted felons would have found the Plain an inviting area with its vast expanse for hit-and-run activities.

Matthew Dean was returning from Devizes Fair when he was attacked by the robbers who pulled him from his horse, rifled his pockets and removed a wallet containing £20 in notes and from another one sovereign and a half in gold and £2 in silver. After their departure Dean, who was unhurt, had recovered his wits sufficiently to give chase and was soon joined by a Mr Morgan, Mr Sainsbury from West Lavington and his neighbour William Hooper from nearby Cornbury Farm.

During the chase across Chitterne Down, one of the attackers, Benjamin Colclough, collapsed and his dead body was discovered the following morning. The others continued to make good their escape but were eventually cornered. They were disarmed of a crowbar, several large 'vossils' (hazel sticks used for sheep pen hurdles) and a handkerchief containing a heavy stone – hardly the tools of a professional highwayman! In gratitude for his assistance Mr Dean, who had recovered most of his loss, gave William Hooper a silver snuff box. Mr Morgan was rewarded by public subscription but no acknowledgement is recorded to Mr Sainsbury for his spirited involvement.

At the subsequent trial at the Devizes Quarter Sessions all three of the remaining robbers were sentenced to transportation to Tasmania for fifteen years. Colclough was buried at Chitterne without funeral rites. A second memorial stone, on Chitterne Down, marks the spot where he died.

The assault upon Matthew Dean was the last such encounter of any note recorded on the Plain. The development of banks in the market towns, in which farmers could deposit the results of their transactions, reduced the need for large sums to be carried personally.

An amusing postscript to this event was provided by Australian soldiers stationed on the Plain during the First World War. Claiming to be descendants of the robbers, they travelled to Imber and chatted amiably with Sydney Dean about the 1839 incident and the subsequent fate of their forebears who had been transported to the opposite end of the globe!

2 Imber reaches Maturity

'Imber . . . is the most isolated of all the villages
on the Plain and the loveliest and most unspoilt'
Ella Noyes.

On 11 February 1793, the *Salisbury and Winchester Journal* recorded an amusing event, surely one of the most unusual incidents in the annals of fox hunting. A fox, being hard pressed by hounds and reaching a stage of near exhaustion, ran into the village of Imber and took refuge under the covering of a well. When attempts were made to get him out the poor creature then fell a hundred feet to the bottom. The bucket was lowered by some of the villagers and he instantly laid hold of it and was drawn up a considerable way before tumbling once more to the bottom. The bucket was lowered a second time and the fox, obtaining a more secure hold, was drawn up safely. When he reached the top the villagers released him and the relieved creature got clear away from the pack.

This story, perhaps, tells us as much about the villagers as about the adventurous fox. Uncowed by the landowning fraternity of the hunt, they showed more sympathy for the creature who shared their rural isolation. Living within such an inbred, tightly-knit society would have led to a more tolerant attitude to the unfortunate or plain eccentric among them. 'Sally Gibbs', for example, was baptized and brought up as a girl but discovered at the age of 14 to be a boy. From then on he assumed male attire and lived as a man leaving children and grandchildren. His employment was irregular and he took to poaching to eke out his unstable lifestyle until 1843 when his death, aged around 77, was reported in the *Bristol Journal*.

Silas Pearce, shepherd to the Deans at Seagram's Farm. In 1900 he married Hannah Meaden and had two children, Emily and Bert. Both families had lived in Imber for many generations.

By 1800 Imber had grown slowly from its medieval population of around 250 into a relatively prosperous village of 330 increasing at a rate of around five a year. Its long seclusion made the community more self-supporting than many, its economy totally underpinned by agriculture.

This took the form of sheep farming on the surrounding chalk downland thinly covered by turf, and arable farming on the lower, more sheltered slopes. The two were interdependent with the sheep enriching the fertile arable land by folding, a process whereby the flocks would be brought down from the hills and enclosed nightly in different areas of the fields. Sheep were valued almost as much for their dung as for their wool – for 'the golden hoof' that could enrich the lightest soil. At Imber the crops were rotated on a four-yearly basis with wheat crops grown in two of the years. A mixture of swedes, kale, rape and turnips was grown in the other two or the ground left to grass.

Life on Salisbury Plain was particularly hard on the shepherd, exposed to all weathers on the open downland, but his importance to the local economy and independence from the immediate control of the farmer put him in a special position. Lambing took place at the worst time of the year, from January onwards, with the folds constructed in downland depressions to protect them from the rain. Shearing, however, took place on the lower ground when the companionable sound of sheep bells must have filled the village. It was the only event, apart from the sheep fairs, when the shepherds found companionship with others. John Britton in *The Beauties of Wiltshire* estimated that at this period there were just under a half a million sheep on Salisbury Plain and the Marlborough Downs. Imber flocks we are told numbered a little under a thousand.

The shepherd's devotion to his flock extended to his dogs which formed so important a part of his daily life. They protected the sheep from predators and guided the flocks many miles along thinly marked tracks. The droves crossing the unenclosed downland were used for the movement of sheep to the numerous pennings available for night shelter or to the great sheep fairs like that at Bratton Camp, famous also as a watering place in all but the driest season. Yarnbury Castle to the south of Imber was another, the position of earlier sheep pens still clearly indicated by low ridges in a rectangular pattern.

In his book *A Shepherd's Life*, W. H Hudson mentioned how well these faithful sheepdogs reciprocated the attachment of their masters. He relates his meeting with the head shepherd of Imber Court. This would have been Sydney Pearce, shepherd to Edward Dean for forty years. He had never owned a dog that he had not acquired as a pup, trained himself, and retained until death. Now retired and living on parish relief, he related to Hudson his great affection for his dogs which he was often compelled to shoot, 'not because he would have found them too great a burden when they had become too old and their senses decayed, but because it was painful to see them in their decline, perpetually craving to be at their old work with the sheep, incapable of doing it any longer, yet miserable if kept from it.'

The village consisted of some fifty cottages in 1800, mud-walled and thatched, mostly situated on the flat ground to the south of the rudimentary track which formed the Warminster to Lavington road. Larger farm buildings, such as Seagrams and Imber Court, a church-owned property, were already leased to the Dean family who were to play such an important role in village life during the ensuing one and a half centuries. By the 1820s they were joined by the Hoopers at Browns Farm, at a time when wheat prices were plummeting and cotton had begun to compete with wool – both factors affecting the village economy. Imber found its relative prosperity undermined and gradually fell into a period of decline. Hard-hit villagers joined the general drift of unemployed labourers seeking work where they could find it, some by joining the army. Despite this trend, neither the Swing Riots at Pythouse, Tisbury nor the Chartist riots at Devizes appear to have had any repercussions at Imber and, surprisingly, in 1851, its population peaked at 440 residents.

By mid-century Imber was learning to adapt to the mechanisation and new farming techniques which were making agriculture marginally more profitable. The new Poor Law, replacing outdoor relief with the new union workhouses, reduced the Poor Rate burden by sending off the destitute to finish their days at Warminster Union. The misery caused to elderly and impoverished villagers who had previously lived cocooned in such a remote community must have been acute. Warminster, the nearest town to Imber, was over six miles distant, its seldom-used track marked only by regular-spaced chalk heaps. Mud or snow on Summer Down Hill made it impassable for wheeled vehicles for much of the year.

Once at Warminster, however, new horizons were opening up by the mid-19th century. In 1856 the Great Western Railway had successfully completed its new line from Chippenham to Salisbury via Warminster forging a vital link with London, Bristol and South Wales. Imber families, previously forced out by starvation, could now hope for a better life elsewhere. Thus from 1850 the village developed the phenomenon of a rising standard of living but a falling population. It seems that as more efficient farming methods reduced the need for labour, migration benefited the job opportunities for those who stayed behind. It was a false Spring. As the 19th century progressed, the agricultural depression of the 1870s and 80s exacerbated the falling population. It was a decline that was to continue until the 1943 evacuation.

A view of the vicarage taken from the tower of St Giles. It was demolished in 1969 following shell damage.

By the mid-19th century Imber had developed a form and character which could have been recognised by any returning Imburian following the Second World War. The Post Office Directory of 1859, for example, records in its routine description a broad perspective:

Imber is a parish in Swanborough hundred, Warminster union, South Wilts. 6 miles east-by-north from Warminster. 7 miles south-east from Westbury Station, and 4 miles north-east-by-east from Heytesbury. 112 miles from London. Diocese of Salisbury, archdeaconry of Wilts, and deanery of Potterne. The living is a perpetual curacy, annual value £112, with residence, in the gift of the Marquis of Bath. The Rev William Dyer is the incumbent. The church of St Giles is a neat edifice, in the Perpendicular style of architecture. In the church are two stone effigies representing Crusaders, also the remains of a

chapel. Here is a national school also a place of worship for Baptists. The
population in 1851 was 440, area in acres 3,033.

There were now around eighty buildings in the village. Most of these
would have been ordinary cottages, but they also included the barns and
other outhouses of the five farms, as well as the church, Baptist Chapel,
School, the Bell Inn, vicarage, Imber Court, smithy and windmill. The
Deans, William and Matthew, were farming at Seagram's and Imber Court
and Henry Hooper at Browns Farm. William Fricker junior had taken over
control of Parsonage Farm from his 84-year old father. Edward Hayter, at
that time landlord of the Bell Inn, also leased the windmill on higher ground
in Carrion Pit Lane to the south. James Cruse, the carrier, when weather

The Revd James Hugh Pearson, vicar of Imber from 1885-1899 with his housekeeper Mrs
Payton and the 'garden boy'. The original photograph belonged to Mrs Bessie May (nee
Cruse) who worked for the vicar as a maid.

permitted, took his creaking wagon across the rough tracks to the markets
at Salisbury every Tuesday, to Warminster on Saturdays and to Devizes on
alternate Thursdays, always returning the same day. William Daniell was
a tailor and shopkeeper. Elijah Meaden, a boot and shoe maker, plied his
trade at the corner of Church Lane. With the exception of the Hayters, these

were all families still represented in the village at the time of the evacuation. Among the agricultural labourers, forming by far the biggest unit on the 1861 Census, were the Pearces, Goddards, Whites and the Naish family. It is possible that the vicar, Reverend William Dyer M.A. and the schoolmistress, Mrs James Staples, were two of a very small number with a vision of life far beyond the confines of the parish.

Brown's Farm in Bungey Lane. The Hooper family farmed here and at Cornbury near Gore's Cross from the 18th century.

And so we are beginning to flesh out the bones. What is needed now is an overview, preferably by a person with an acute eye for rural detail. Ella Noyes, tramping the dusty tracks in the 1890s, preparing notes for her subsequent book on Salisbury Plain, provides us with such a picture:

> The village lies in a deep fold of the Plain, on the track of another little winter stream; on all sides the slopes of the high downs surround it. It is just one straggling street of old cottages and farmsteads, winding along the hollow under the sheltering elms; the narrow stream brims fresh and clear through it in spring, leaving its bed dry, to fill up with coarse grass and weeds in summer. The white-washed cottages, with their leaning timbers and deep thatched roofs, are set down in short rows and groups, the angles and nooks between them filled in with garden plots full of flowers: rose bushes, here and there a

Granny Staples Shop. It was the oldest domestic building in the village and situated in a jumble of cottages known as the Barracks near Tinker's Farm. The shop was burnt down during the First World War. By this time the Staples were both dead.

lilac, lilies, and tangles of everlasting peas. There is an old timbered house about midway along the street which cannot be younger than the fourteenth century. Such barns too, there are, deep, lofty, capacious, built of grand old timbers, with a thick cape of thatch thrown over the long roof and two pockets in the thatch bulging out over the big double storied doors. The long walls of the orchards and gardens are all the old mud built kind here, rustic and comfortable under their coping of thatch.

The ancient timbered house would almost certainly have been the shop of John and Eliza Staples. The summer growth of coarse weeds and grass in the brook may well have given rise to the colloquial description of the troublesome stream as 'Imber Dock'.

Opposite page: Andrew and Caroline Davis outside their home at the Dring, the most westward stretch of the Imber main street. Mr Davis was recorded as an agricultural labourer and a Baptist deacon in 1886.

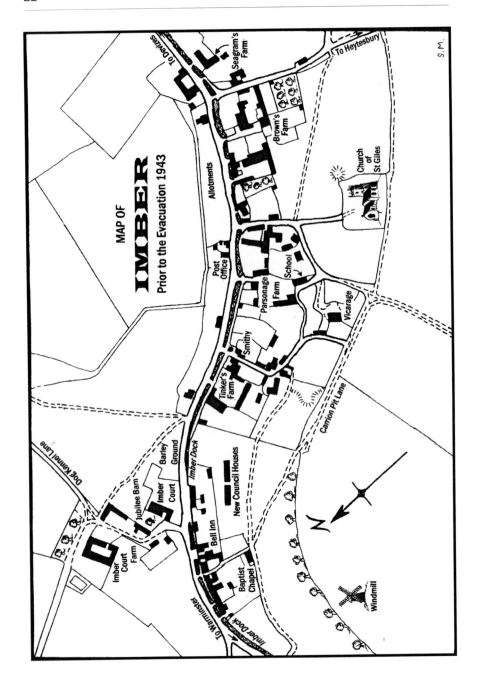

MAP OF
IMBER
Prior to the Evacuation 1943

3 A Village Tour

In the early 1970s Major Gordon Revels produced an Imber guide while stationed for two years at Warminster. Tragically, he died shortly afterwards and would have seen little of the fruits of his labour. It is full of interesting detail both of the church and of village life in general. The route that he took for his perambulation is basically the one we shall follow in this chapter using the opportunity to delve a little further into its history and the people who lived there during the 19th and early 20th centuries.

Although not central to its parish, the church of St Giles, overlooking the area from the southern slopes, is a good starting point for any survey of Imber. Dating from the 13th and 14th centuries, it is believed to have been built on the site of a much earlier Norman church. This handsome stone and tiled building, with its rectangular tower, has seen many changes appropriate to the needs of the time. The aisle windows, for example, were widened in the l5th century to let in more light, and a stairway added to the tower. The first chancel, shown in Buckler's early-19th century water-colour, had lancet windows but was rebuilt in 1849 for its patron Lord Bath with Perpendicular style windows. In 1895 the church received a further extensive restoration increasing its seating capacity to 200. The church has outlived all else. Today it remains, stripped of its internal fittings, many of which found homes at Edington and other local churches, as the only functional building left. Protected by peerless fencing, it has been in use each year for the September services when families of former inhabitants return to tend their graves and meet with old friends.

North of the church lies the main thoroughfare, its narrow track passing westwards to the town of Warminster and eastwards across the Plain

St Giles Church 1894. You can see the tombs in the side chapel and the churchwarden's box pew in the corner. At that time it would have been occupied by Robert Dean. After the Victorian restoration of the church it was re-dedicated on 30 January 1896 by John Wordsworth, Bishop of Salisbury.

to meet the Devizes Road at Gore Cross. Until the early 20th century it was marked by little more than chalk and whitewashed stones known as Wiltshire lamps which were set up in the turf. Nevertheless, the carrier and other lonely travellers pursuing this elementary route would have been grateful for any assistance. A visitor arriving from the east would have seen the tower of St Giles from a distance as a welcoming sign that his journey was near its end. Soon the gaunt frame of Seagram's Farm would become visible on the left with the date of an extension, 1880, on the gable-end facing down the village. The farm was leased by the Seagram family to Matthew Dean, whose infamous attack by robbers in 1839 was detailed earlier. In 1871, William Robert Dean of Seagram's married Harriet Hooper from nearby Brown's Farm, thus linking the two most prominent Imber families.

Seagram's (or East) Farm. It was leased for several generations by the Dean family. On the gable was a stone carved with the cipher of William Heathcote Seagram dated 1800

Beyond Seagram's (or East) Farm lies Bungey Lane, along the southern route into the village from Heytesbury four and a half miles away. Such a name deserves some explanation. It is believed to have derived from Bungey, a farmer's dog, whose skin was preserved and used as a butter container! One summer there was a glut of butter and, wishing to preserve as

William Robert Dean (1839-1909), from Seagram's Farm. He was always known as Robert, and was the grand-son of Matthew Dean who was attacked by robbers.

much as possible, the villagers filled up every available vessel. This included Bungey's skin which was then hung up in the kitchen. When winter came and fires were lit the butter began to drip. The children are reputed to have stood beneath it chanting 'Drop on my bread, Bungey!' The inhabitants of Imber became known as 'Bungeys' after this intriguing incident.

Along this lane lay Brown's Farm, the home of the Hooper family who had arrived in the area during the 18th century from Brinkworth in north Wiltshire. Associated largely with Cornbury Farm near Gore Cross (as they are today), it was William Pearce Hooper who rented Brown's Farm for a considerable time until his death in 1902. Two years later his brother James was able to purchase the property from the Church Commissioners and the family continued to farm it until the evacuation. At that time it was occupied by Captain Arthur Williams who was married to Hilda Hooper. Her brother, Charlie Hooper, the owner, was then living at Deptford (near Wylye). Pictures taken in the garden of Brown's show the Williams' great fondness for their horses and dogs.

From Bungey's Lane a track turned to the left. This was known as 'Postman's Path' from its early use by the mailmen who walked daily, often in the foulest weather, from the village of Codford, via Chitterne, a journey of some seven miles. After delivering the mail at around 9 am and clearing the letterbox the postman sheltered in a tin hut at the western end of the High Street. During the day he would perform odd jobs around the village before returning with the outgoing mail at 4.20 pm (or 3.50 pm in winter). Postmen, including the fondly remembered Edward Parker from Codford, continued this long journey by foot and, later, bicycle for many years, often blowing a whistle to let villagers know they had arrived. On one occasion the postman was attacked by an owl. On another during a period of heavy snow in 1880 he is recorded as walking over the top of a lambing pen without knowing it and could not return to his village for two days.

Imber Post Office. Opened for the first time in 1909. Before that mail was brought by a postman from Codford St Mary, via Chitterne. Ellen and John Carter (shown in the picture) ran the business for the entire period until the evacuation.

In 1909 a post office was opened in Imber. It is remembered as little more than a hut built on the sparse northern stretch of the High Street, its path lined with masses of *Iris Reticulata*. A reporter from the *Post Office Magazine* found the experience of visiting it quite daunting:

Imber claims to be the loneliest village in England. This may be challenged, but having just returned from a visit to its Post Office, I must say it is the loneliest hamlet I have yet seen for it is in the middle of the Salisbury Plain and its attendant downs, and they make up the most lonely and empty of all the plains in England . . The Post Office is in a quaint cottage in its one straggling 'street' and in the charge of Mrs M L Carter, England's loneliest postmistress. I introduced myself and was at once met with, 'I know. You wrote about the South Stack postman and described how he had to climb up and down over four hundred steps. We are exposed to severe gales here and our postman has to cycle against buffeting winds seven miles each way with a heavy load. But he is always cheerful, and on particularly bad days he comes in with a chuckle saying, "If that South Stack fellow can stick it, I recon' a bit of a gale won't hurt me!"'

Kelly's Directory shows John Carter to have been its first and only sub postmaster but it was his wife, Ellen, who took most responsibility. John was a carpenter with his premises adjacent to the post office. Together they became the first in the village to own a telephone – Imber 1! The early doctors to serve the village also walked the distance from Codford although one had the benefit of a gig.

Church Lane 1909. In this picture you are looking across the allotments to Stocks Arch, the entrance to Church Lane. On the right is the home and workshop of the shoemaker Harry Meaden and his wife Charlotte.

Returning to the village High Street we find the Imber Dock flowing along the southern side and bridged at various points. One of these junctions was known as Stocks Arch. It crossed into Church Street where a row of cottages fronted it to the right. An early-20th century photograph shows a further row of thatched and whitewashed cottages along the High Street near here with a well outside one of them and the village post box set into the wall. Previous to the opening of the post office this was the only mail collection point and is first noted in a directory of 1875. John Cruse is reputed to have lived in the adjacent cottage for a time. A man of quick temper he is alleged on one tempestuous occasion to have swept up the china dishes from the table and thrown them down the well from whence they were never recovered!

Stocks Arch. The turning on the left, past the children, leads to the church. In the first house lived Ann Pearce and next to her lived 'Widow Pearce' (no relation) who sold sweets and oil. Lily Marsh (later Adlam) is the girl on the left.

There were few buildings, other than the post office, along the northern side of the High Street. The Nag's Head lay opposite the entrance to Bungey Lane near two cottages later inhabited by Enos and Fanny Matthews. There is no written evidence to confirm its original purpose as an inn although this is probably the case. Between here and the centre of the village were allotments, half acre strips of land enabling villagers to supplement their meagre wages.

Cottages in Church Lane with the vicarage beyond. Mrs William Nash, widow of the blacksmith (Albert's uncle) lived in the left hand cottage. One of the girls standing in the road is
Lily Meaden.

Leaving the High Street at Stocks Arch we ascend Church Street once
more to St Giles's Church, its embattled five-pinnacled tower displayed to
good effect. A pastoral scene photographed early in the 20th century shows
the Ruddle family standing in front of their brick and flint residence to the
left of the churchyard entrance. Mrs Ruddle, with her three children, stands

View of Imber from the downs. On the skyline can be seen the old windmill. The lines of
clothes hung out to dry would indicate it was washing day! James and Eliza Daniels lived
at 'No 7 Imber', the house with smoke coming from the chimney.

The Imber windmill was situated on the down above Carrion Pit Lane. It was customary for the cottage folk to take their gleanings there for grinding; barley meal for their pigs and wheat flour for their own use. Members of the Cruse family are standing in front. The mill was eventually demolished before the First World War.

solemnly displayed beside a rose-covered wall with lark cages hanging by the windows. The Carter twins whose father was the church sexton, stand demurely to the right.

Church Street divides at this point. The muddy track which skirts the graveyard led into the hills and was hailed by the rather macabre name of Carrion Pit Lane. Here would be found, high on Chapel Down, a chalk pit, a dew pond and a windmill. Elderly residents have recorded their memories of leazing (gleaning) and taking the corn 'Up Carpet' (a corruption of the words Carrion Pit) to be milled. The barley was fed to the pigs and the wheat used to make bread. Recalling her long life, Bertha Knight (née Meaden), aged 90 in 1967 remembered many youthful visits to the mill. Her father, Henry Meaden, was the village boot and shoe maker, in season helping to shear the huge flocks of Imber sheep. She recalled her mother baking her own bread in a small brick oven:

> We children often went to the windmill to fetch flour from the miller so that our mothers could bake bread once a week. Not all villagers were able to do this – many of the dwellings were simply mud houses – so they bought bread from neighbours who did, at a halfpenny a loaf'.

A succession of millers, including the landlord of the Bell Inn and members of the Dean family, controlled the windmill until decay led to its closure and eventual demolition before the First World War.

Returning to take the lower track beneath the downland, we find the imposing structure of Imber Vicarage to our left. This large stone residence occasionally hosted social gatherings, although the incumbent and his family were often looked down on by the local gentry. The vicar needed to be hardy to visit his outlying parishioners in such a remote and weather-torn area, while his family relied greatly on their own company and amusements.

Miss Clara Mountford, a schoolmistress, with her dog Nellie. She came from the Bluecoat School, Birmingham whilst the Revd Charles Watling (1899-1917) was the Imber vicar.

Across the lane from the Vicarage lay the National School established in 1836. An earlier Sunday School is mentioned in 1814 when attendance was a condition set for receiving poor relief from the overseer. The National School was enlarged to take 60 pupils from 1876 although its average attendance in 1889 was only 32. Here a succession of schoolmistresses struggled to fulfil the conditions under which government grants were paid affecting both their salaries and the maintenance of the school. These were awarded to the school managers on the basis of regular attendance and a satisfactory report from the School Inspector at the dreaded annual inspection.

One such mistress was Rebecca Pocock who lodged at the vicarage with the Rev Charles Morgan Watling and his wife in the early twentieth century. Becky was a popular teacher who became romantically involved with Bob Hooper from Brown's Farm, with the Watlings acting as match-makers. After an evening party at the Vicarage at which she sang 'The Last Rose of Summer', he proposed marriage and was accepted. They lived and worked at Cornbury, the Hooper's farm near Gore Cross. At the Imber Service Day in 1981, an old resident, Mrs Shale, recalled that Miss Pocock taught her wonderfully well. When asked by her grandson where she had been educated she replied 'Imber University'. The child told his school teacher who decided he must have meant Edinburgh University!

Another popular teacher in the 1920s was Ivy Holliday from West Lavington. She was newly qualified and came temporarily owing to the illness of the usual mistress. Cycling daily across the downs, she was initially nervous at the prospect of teaching boys, but the pupils of Imber proved to be some of the most pleasant she ever taught. Eventually she was offered a permanent position in the school but refused it in order to gain more experience elsewhere.

Beyond the school lay Parsonage Farm, run for almost all the the 18th and 19th centuries by the Fricker family who were generous benefactors in the village. Beyond here, in a strange jumble of cottages, known as the Barracks, which was probably the hub of the village, lay the oldest domestic residence. Shown in a beautiful painting by Bernard Gotch recently displayed in Salisbury Museum, it was a thatched and white-walled property with a massive timber lintel supporting a slight overhang above the door. This was the grocery and provision shop of Eliza Staples, later referred to as 'Granny', and her husband James. The Staples, father and son, had been three generations of blacksmiths from 1745 working from a smithy shown at the side of the house. One unnamed member of this family invented a metal turn-farrow for a plough which was marketed by Reeves, the agricultural engineering firm at Bratton. Emma, a daughter of James and Eliza's, is recorded as playing the new harmonium in the church when the old gallery used by earlier church musicians was finally removed. She is also shown in the 1891 Census to have taught needlework in the school. During the First World War the house was destroyed by fire. Thomas Tinnams raised

Parsonage House. The farm, situated in the centre of the village, was run for almost all the 18th and 19th centuries by members of the Fricker family. It was then taken over by the Deans. Frank Meaden is believed to be the man on the left. Next is Fanny, daughter of the blacksmith William Nash, Jabez Early and his daughter Jenny and, possibly, Wilfred Dean on the right, leaning on the fence. Stuart Carter was the occupier at the evacuation in 1943.

Mr A.G.Hartley, seated here in front of Parsonage House, came regularly from London. He was a generous benefactor of the village and came down for the shooting. The lady on the right is Mrs Gladys Dean wife of the farmer Sydney Dean.

Eliza Staples, known in her later years as 'Granny', outside her grocery and provisions shop. Her husband James was the last of three generations of blacksmiths working from the smithy at the side of the shop.

the alarm and William Meaden helped to fight the flames but to no avail. Fortunately, by this time Granny Staples was dead and the old house empty. Her husband had pre-deceased her in 1888. The thriving blacksmith business was taken over by William Nash whose nephew Albert continued to run it until forced to leave in 1943.

Returning to the main street, we find the road curves gently left westwards past Tinker's Farm. Imber farms are confusing, being known by different names, in this case South, or Imber Farm, at various periods. Tinker's Farm, with its large thatched barn, was shown on the 1838 Tithe Map to be owned by a family of that name who had been freeholders for some 300 years. Photographs show a large rectangular building with jutting wings joined by a verandah. It was enclosed by a cast iron fence along the front. By the 20th century this, too, had come into the hands of the Deans who leased out the farmhouse to a succession of tenants.

Tinker's Farm before 1911. It was previously known as Imber Farm. The road on the left is Barracks lane.

We are now at the western end of the village with 'Barley Field' on the northern side. This is the name given to the only flat open space available, a recreational area well suited to communal activities such as cricket which was a popular pastime. It was also a rallying point for political or religious itinerants. Pictures from early in the 20th century show a more organised revivalist meeting held there by a Mr and Mrs Ware. This was probably run by a nonconformist Bible group. There is a text-covered living van, a large canvas marquee for meetings and a smaller candy-striped enclosure presumably for the sale of religious tracts. All are contained within a hurdle enclosure. The presence of neatly-attired worshippers as well as

View of the main street from west to east before the First World War. Granny Staples house is shown on the right.

View of the main street from east to west before the First World War. The row of cottages has the Imber post box let into the wall just beyond the well. From the left the cottages were occupied by the Goddards, Edward Meaden, the Bundys and Harry Daniels. The winterbourne known as Imber Dock is shown in a dry condition to the right.

Imber took great pride in its cricket teams which used to play on the Barley Field. In this picture, taken in the early 1920s, we can see in the back row: Wilfred Dean, Willie Carter, Albert Nash, Ted Dean and Georgie Atkins. In the centre row are: Leslie Dean, Fred Dean, Tom Dean, Sid Dean and Stan Harrington. In the front row are Buffy (Charles) Meaden and Arthur Goddard. Shown faintly in the back row is Mr Price who brought the beer!

Mr and Mrs Ware's Missionary Meeting took place on the Barley Ground around 1909. As you can see, it was well attended.

children, domestic servants and shepherds newly returned from the fields would indicate that the interest shown was fairly wide. Indeed, the visitation lasted for a fortnight and the vicar, Revd Charles Watling, announced his displeasure from the pulpit because his flock went straight to the meeting tent after leaving his church!

Occasionally evangelical groups would come to preach the Gospel like this one led by Mr and Mrs Ware around 1909. There is a text-covered van in front of the tent, domestic servants to the right and shepherds returning from the downs behind them. The event continued for about two weeks – much to the displeasure of the vicar!

Immediately adjacent to Barley Field was the manor house, a substantial ivy-covered mansion. Imber Court had been largely rebuilt along more elegant lines in the mid-18th century. The Wadman family, who also owned Tinhead Court near Edington, lived in comparative affluence there during the 17th and 18th centuries renting the property from the church authorities. Tradition has it that one of the Wadman family haunted the premises holding a lighted candle before her. At the kennels, too, it was held that chains could be heard rattling and dogs howling, presumably the ghosts of hunting dogs once used for coursing. The children were told, 'If you hear chains rattling don't be frightened, tis only the ghosts!' John Wadman founded a charity in the village with a bequest of £40 in 1688 which continued into the 20th century.

Imber Court before the fire in 1920. The Wadmans leased it from the Dean and Chapter of Salisbury Cathedral for a long period before the Dean tenancy. The Tucker family also ran 'an Academy for Young Gentlemen' from here in the 19th century. After Edward Dean's long tenancy, it was purchased by Thomas Holloway in 1920. During renovations, it was destroyed by fire, but rebuilt shortly afterwards.

Subsequent to the Wadmans residence of Imber Court, Richard Tucker from Broadwindsor near Bridport ran 'an academy for young gentlemen' from there with the aid of two of his sons, Robert and John . The school was held in the stables which had a large bell on the roof later used by the Deans to summon the groom.

The Dean family claim a close kinship with King John through his mistress Mollie, whose son became Earl of Gloucester. The first mention of the family at Imber appears in the parish records in 1783. Although it is not clear when they first began their long residence of Imber Court, one section of the family farmed both Imber Court Farm and Southdown, another large farm close to the Bratton Road. Edward Dean – grandson of the spirited Matthew who was robbed near Gore Cross – farmed here for much of the second half of the 19th century. Although a man of high moral probity, he was not averse to visiting the Bell Inn. On one occasion, when returning home a little tipsy, he missed his footing and finished up in Imber Dock which was then in full spate. Fortunately Jemima Meaden, living in an adjacent cottage, witnessed the accident. She called a neighbour and ran with her clothes prop from the washing line to fish him from the water, thus saving him from being swept under the road and possibly drowning. At that time all the work was done with teams of horses; there were no tractors until after the First World War. Farm wagons took the corn along the rutted tracks to Warminster and came back loaded with coal. The Deans provided one churchwarden, and sometimes two, in almost unbroken succession from 1791 throughout the ensuing years, an unprecented record of village service for one family.

The Bell Inn looking towards Warminster. A stone on the gable end has the date 1769 and the initials 'PF', probably referring to Philip Flower overseer of the poor at that time.

By this time on our tour we would have been well in need of refreshment, our throats no doubt inflamed by the dustiness of the Imber lanes. Crossing the road to the southern side, almost opposite the turning to the complex of farming units that was Imber Court Farm, we find the Bell Inn, its sign swinging in the breeze. Over the gable end of the inn (which had been built originally as a private house) is inscribed 'PF 1769', a reference to Philip Flower overseer of the poor at that time, a duty he shared with Thomas Wort. The inn (as it became) had replaced an earlier one recorded in the Tithe Survey of 1838 as being on the other side of the road to the west of a field called 'Bell Living'. At that time John Hayter, a farmer, held the licence as publican, a labour he continued in the new premises until his death, aged 80, in 1859. He was succeeded by his son Edward until his retirement sometime after 1875, a long occupancy by one family.

The west end of the village known as 'The Dring'. In the first cottage lived Arthur Goddard, next was Bert Potter (a retired policeman), and then Andrew Davis. Percy Daniels
(shown in the picture) lived in a house that stood further back. He was the father of Phyllis
Daniels whose marriage to Bernard Wright was celebrated just before the evacuation.

Having been suitably refreshed, we complete our journey, as we
started, by visiting a place of worship. Just past the Bell Inn a track led off
to the left up to the Baptist Chapel which stood well back from the High
Street and was fronted by its own small graveyard. The chapel was a long
rectangular building cob-built but with brick foundations. Its presence was
a clear reminder of the strong nonconformist element to be found at Imber.

Of the countless shepherds who had walked the Plain, only a few
have left their mark. One such was David Saunders from West Lavington,
'the Shepherd of Salisbury Plain', who became a hero of popular religious
literature in the 18th century. David Saunders was an evangelist whose
inspirational preaching led to the formation of local Christian groups of
young men. He often preached at Imber where groups of dissenters met in
private homes.

John Saffery, minister of the Brown Street Baptist Chapel at Salisbury,
was married to a member of the reforming Whitaker family at Bratton. He,
too, was a man of evangelical zeal encouraging the creation of meeting
houses in the surrounding area , including Imber, as adjuncts of the chapel
at Bratton. His enthusiasm for preaching at these local village 'stations' was
soon followed by others who walked vast distances, rode horses, gigs and –
later – cycled to these outposts. The Bratton chapel even preserved a special

fund for 'horse-hire in village preaching'. Marjorie Reeves, in her book *Sheep Bell and Ploughshare*, relates an amusing incident that occurred to three Baptist worthies driving back from a Sunday evening service at Imber in a pony and trap. On the steep downward road one observed to the others, 'Whose is that wheel running down the hill in front? Why, 'tis ours!'

The Baptist chapel. Situated to the rear of the Bell Inn, the chapel was fronted by its own graveyard which is still protected by the army. It was built in the 1830s by the Imber Baptist fraternity after they had broken away from the chapel at Bratton. It also included its own school.

The interior of the Baptist chapel. Some preachers walked miles to take services there. Harry Meaden, the shoemaker and chapel elder, took services accompanied by his small dog. From 1907 until the evacuation in 1943, the chapel services were regularly taken by Frank Maidment the minister at Chitterne who, in his younger days, cycled there in all weathers.

In 1839 the thriving Baptist community from Imber broke away from that at Bratton at the request of village elders Thomas Found, James Pearce, Isaac Carter and William Grant, despite reservations from the Bratton congregation. They then constructed their own chapel using voluntary labour. Stone was brought back from the hills by shepherds and farmhands. Women brought pails of water to the site whilst their menfolk mixed the mortar. Later, in 1868, the chapel was repaired and partly re-built for the thriving congregation. By this time it incorporated a British (i.e. nonconformist) school. Warburton's *Census of Wiltshire Schools 1859* states that 'three parts of the [Imber] population are dissenters'. The British School was then catering for 50-70 scholars in crowded chapel rooms at a time when the National School had only 20-30.

Joseph Goddard was perhaps the best known of all the Imber ministers, his story later recorded by the Revd Erskine Rankin, a luminary of the Baptist church. Joseph, an agricultural labourer, was a deacon of the Imber chapel and a lay preacher sought after by congregations over a wide area. He used to say towards the end of his life that he had walked 8,000 miles over the Plain to preach the Gospel. During his period of influence at Imber we are told that for 17 years there had not been a single criminal case brought before the local courts. Lloyd George, already a well known political figure, was told of this remarkable fact by a Warminster magistrate whom he had visited. He was sufficiently impressed to wish to meet the preacher.

> The magistrate drove him to Imber and knocked on the door of Joseph Goddard's cottage. His wife answered and in reply to a request to see him was told, "E baint in, sir. 'E be gone to Warminster'.
>
> 'This is Mr Lloyd George', said the magistrate, 'he would like to see Mr Goddard.' The reply was very short. 'Ah. He is a Member of Parliament.' Again the short 'Ah. He is a Baptist.' Mrs Goddard then thrust out her hand saying, 'Then we be brother and sister.' Gripping her hand the famous statesman said, 'Yes, we are madam.' She looked him straight in the eye and said, 'We shall meet in heaven bye and bye.' Mr Lloyd George, with tears in his eyes, replied, 'By the grace of God, we will.'

4 Gathering Clouds

Imber must have seemed an idyllic place for a child at the beginning of the 20th century when Dorothy Webb grew up there. The daughter of a journeyman baker who worked in premises adjacent to the Bell Inn in an area known as the Dring, she was only three weeks old when they arrived in 1907. It was still a purely agricultural community growing acres of corn and tending large flocks of sheep. Dorothy grew up with a surprising degree of

Imber. A sketch by Bernard Gotch for W.H.Hudson's book A Shepherd's Life at the beginning of the 20th century.

45

freedom roaming the Plain far and wide, its air full of the sound of peewits and bleating sheep. Tracks marked by the little heaps of chalk and the five-pinnacled tower of St Giles's Church, guided her home. But as the century progressed the activities of the army, which had laid claim to the Plain in 1897, became more intrusive. During the First World War military operations in the area increased considerably and shells from the surrounding artillery ranges damaged several of the cottages. Dorothy, and others like her, could no longer wander at will across the downland. Red flags warned of large areas too dangerous for rambling.

Other, underlying factors, were also disturbing the fabric of the village. Like most other Salisbury Plain villages, Imber was continuing to lose its population. From a peak of 440 in 1851 it had dropped to 261 at the beginning of the new century. Agricultural depression, compounded by mechanisation and free trade policies, had affected all rural areas. American wheat and Australian mutton and wool dominated the market. At Imber the workforce was steadily cut back and general improvements in agricultural efficiency were made. Farming was diversified to include dairying and crops other than grain. Young men, sorely in need of work, left to join the army or to seek work in the surrounding towns, the girls to join the growing tide of domestic servants. Families seeking a more secure base disappeared into the surrounding villages or much further afield to the colonies. Families like that of Jim Earley. He was one of nine children, the son of a noted dewpond maker, Jabez Earley. Jim was forced to leave his young family and walk each week to Norton Bavant for farm employment. In 1907, when accommodation was available, the family moved from Imber to join him there.

But such considerations would have meant little to Dorothy the baker's daughter. Her early memories are of a golden village full of warm neighbourliness and simple pleasures, the surrounding downland suffused by the never-ending song of larks:

> Looking back now I realise that Imber was a paradise for children. We had few toys or books, no cinemas or tv but we were never bored as there were so many exciting things going on outside... As the seasons came round there was sheep shearing to watch, then the harvest when every hand was called on to help. We loved to go gleaning the ears of corn left after the rake had

A view of Imber early in the 20th century taken from the church tower, looking towards Parsonage and Tinker's Farms. Note the abundance of trees that can be seen at that time.

been round. What a feast for the hens when we came home, tired out and bitten all over by harvest bugs. A gate in the wall of our garden led into a field where cows grazed and here we wandered at will bird-nesting or picking cowslips to make tossy-balls.

Pamela Tennant, a member of the Glenconner family, was also a child at that time and remembered driving with her parents to see this strange village on the downs and to visit an old lady who had a reputation for curing birds suffering from the 'gapes'. People would bring their poultry to her from miles around. The old lady approached the family along her garden path, her face a mass of little wrinkles and smiles eager to impart a vision she had recently had following a serious illness:

As I lay there, I see'd 'en come suddenly out o' the darkness. Great gold letters at the foot of my bed! And I tried to read 'en but couldn't because I was that weak, and all the letters kep' jigging up and down, and were so bright it was most I could do to keep my eyes on 'en. But there! I was so ill, they all on 'en thought I could do nothen' but die. Most partickler ill I was; and I lay there just not able to speak when I see'd 'en come shining out 'o the dark. Great nine inch letters, I should say. And all glittery gold! An' I prayed to myself, 'O God! Help me read Thy message; for I'm turr'ble weak; help me read it' and suddenly I see the words 'Thou shalt NOT DIE, but LIVE'. Those were

the very words I read, great nine inch letters, all gold, at the foot o' my bed...
Then with a most happy laugh, 'And, I didn't die! I lived! I lived!'

For special village celebrations the huge three-bay corn barn at Imber
Court Farm was ideal, being the largest enclosed space available. The central
portion, used for threshing the corn, had huge double doors on either side.
When open they provided the draught to separate the grain from the chaff

Whitmonday at Imber outside the school. Probably the occasion of a Slate Club Feast Day.
The boys are carrying red and white spotted handkerchiefs containing a knife, fork and
plate for their lunch in the barn.

and to allow entry for the farm wagons to unload directly into the side bays.
The churchwardens' account book tells of the two memorable occasions when
Queen Victoria's jubilees were celebrated. In 1887, for instance;

> This being the 50th year of our Gracious Majesty Queen Victoria's reign,
> the celebration of her Jubilee took place in the parish of Imber on 30th May
> 1887. £23 13s. 10d. was raised by subscription. It being Whit Monday the club
> paraded the village attended by the West Lavington Brass Band. A dinner
> was provided at Mr E Dean's barn, consisting of cold beef and mutton (334
> lbs of meat) 30 hot plum puddings, 20 gallons of bread and 72 gallons of ale.

Including visitors, some 360 persons dined together, the meat and puddings
being prepared in the kitchens of Imber Court by Kate Dean and her maids.
Entertainments then took place at Barley Field, the adjoining recreation

Imber Coronation Committee 1911. It was formed to organise the activities celebrating the Coronation of King George V.

area. Conjuring tricks by Dr Seaton, foot races, donkey races, dancing and other amusements were recorded and the whole village gaily decorated with evergreen and flowers with several garlanded archways erected over the streets. Similarly, for the Queen's Diamond Jubilee ten years later the barn housed 340 guests for its feast with a cricket match and tug-of-war among the subsequent entertainment – the honours being shared with teams from Shrewton.

The 1911 Coronation celebrations photographed at the Jubilee barn where a dinner was held. A number of celebrities, including the Hon. Geoffrey Howard the local M.P. for the Westbury Division, attended.

Such high days and holidays were continued into the 20th century. The celebrations for the Coronation of Edward VII were meticulously prepared by a Coronation Committee photographed for the occasion. Peeping from the back of the group is Harry Meaden the village shoemaker, obviously in lighter mood. He was a chapel elder who took the services accompanied by his small dog but was said to restrict his teetotal beliefs to Sundays! At the festivities to honour the Silver Jubilee of George V in 1935 an incident threatened the proceedings. A bonfire was arranged on the hillside above. In order to encourage the flames, a tripod was built above the pile. On it was placed a barrel of tar, the idea being that the burning pitch would drip down on the fire. Unfortunately the supports burnt through and the flaming tar barrel rolled down the hill on to the Barley Field below to the alarm of the waiting spectators.

At the beginning of the 20th century Edward Dean was continuing the long residency of his family at Imber Court where entertainments tended to reflect the pursuits of the upper classes. Dances, card games and tennis parties

Edward Henry Dean (1842-1910) who lived and farmed from Imber Court. He is shown with his wife Kate and their children Tom, Gladys and Kathleen.

Fred, Sydney and Tom Dean with Mr A.G.Hartley, 1902. Mr Hartley rented Parsonage Farm and held shooting parties over the fields followed by high tea with Devizes cheese cakes as the main delicacy.

were popular, with cricket matches on the adjoining Barley Field. Entries in the diary of Thomas Stone from Market Lavington highlight the strong passion for field sports. Thomas was first cousin once removed of William Pearce Hooper and learning to shoot prior to emigrating to California. During visits to Brown's Farm in 1895 he recorded his daily bag including rooks, wood pigeons, doves and even lapwing despite the continuing presence of toothache which he attempted to cure by compacting the hollowed tooth with sawdust. Gladys Dean, Edward's daughter, in her diary mentioned even grander affairs at Imber Court, particularly partridge shoots of large proportions. At Ladywell, a small farm by the junction of the Warminster and Bratton roads, rabbit shoots were organised by the Deans with 3,000 being bagged in a day.

The family Christmas festivities are also recorded by Gladys Dean:

On Christmas Eve the school children came carol singing and were all given one penny each. Then the grown ups came and sang carols about midnight,

Robert Dean shown in the conservatory at Seagram's where he farmed until his death in 1909. In 1871 he had married Harriet Hooper, thus joining together the two most prominent farming families in Imber. They had five children including Sydney who later took over the farm.

they brought their harmonium and a violin. Edward used to put a bottle of gin in the boot house for them to drink. When they finished the head man said 'A Merry Christmas to the Master and Mistress and family, likewise the servants.' Then the Mummers came, all dressed up. On Christmas Eve we opened a large hamper which Uncle Herbert Larder sent from London full of presents and fruits. It was sent to Warminster and brought back with the coal. Once the hunt came [when] the fox took refuge in the pantry. The reynard couldn't be found but there was plenty of scent in the house and the hounds would not go away. Eventually he was found.'

Edward Dean's brother Robert, married to Harriet Hooper, farmed at Seagram's at the eastern end of the village where flood water occasionally broke through into the drawing room. Nearby Harriet's brother William Pearce Hooper was farming at Brown's. William was the centre of a host of Hoopers, the descendants of farmers who had lived in the Lavington, Tilshead and Imber area for generations. Pictures show him as a genial, rotund gentleman, spectacled and bewhiskered. When Elizabeth, his wife, died in 1879, it was his cousin Marion Pile who took over, devoting her life to the welfare of his five children.

The children of Robert and Harriet
Dean: Willie (b. 1872), Fred (b.1875),
Frank (b.1874) and Ted (b.1877).
Sydney, the last child, was born later
in 1884.

Imber in flood, January 1911. Seagram's Farm can be seen in the centre of the picture with
Brown's Farm to the right. At the time of the evacuation in 1943, the houses on the left
were occupied by Enos and Fanny Matthews and the Marsh family.

Elizabeth Hooper, wife of William Pearce Hooper, was the daughter of a Tilshead vet. She is shown with their children Agnes (on the donkey), Henry, Robert and John. Another son, William, was born later. After her death in 1879, Marion Pile, William's cousin, became house-keeper and brought up the children.

William Pearce Hooper (1839-1902) who rented Brown's Farm from the Duke of Cleveland's estate. Two years after his death, his brother James Hooper purchased the farm when it came up for sale for £4,300.

Although there were several smaller farms in the village, it was the farming hegemony of these two families, the Deans and the Hoopers, which continued to oversee and influence the village economy right up to the evacuation in 1943. Gladys described the difficulties of farming at Imber prior to the First World War. Rutted tracks made by the horse-drawn wagons had to be kept in repair with flints gathered off the land when activities on the farms were quieter. Horse riders took the shortest route often along ancient tracks made visible only by the large chalk heaps. On one occasion her brother Tom went missing:

> Tom had ridden to Edington for a night out with friends but when he tried to ride home he got lost in the fog. His horse wanted to go one way and Tom decided that it was not the right direction. In the end they were really lost and

Tom lay down under a hayrick with the reins on his arm. The groom came to Imber Court and reported that Master Tom's horse had come back with no sign of his rider. What a to do!! After an hour or two Tom arrived whistling down the road, having walked home.

In those early 20th century days all farming operations were done with teams of horses; there were no tractors at Imber until after the First World War. Farm wagons took the corn to Warminster and came back loaded with coal for the villagers. Ploughing was with two horse teams walking around ten miles a day in all weathers. The men were expected to carry sacks of wheat 2½ cwt apiece. Neither was the lot of women any easier. At Southdown Farm the carter's wife had twenty children, the arrival of each described as 'another bit of love!' With the most basic of domestic facilities at such a remote spot, life must have been very hard, but there would have been little time for reflection for the carter's wife.

It was the vast flocks of sheep whose activities governed all. The life of an arable farm revolved around the sheep – the animals with 'the Golden Hoof'. They were the prime concern of the farm and the source of fertility; before the use of artificial manures they were an integral part of the rotation of crops. The sheep were folded in hurdles to fertilise the village fields by night, while by day the ewes, mostly Hampshire Down sheep, were minded by the shepherd as they grazed on the downs.

Thomas Carter, born in 1877, recorded in old age his memories of the lambing season with 'the shepherds searching the dark downs with lanterns and stoves roaring in their cottages all night ready to warm and revive chilled or ailing lambs'. The shepherd usually had his mobile home near his sheep and this had to be drawn up by horses to the designated spot close to the pens. Constructed at the Bratton Iron Works, these huts were little more than timber-framed sheds mounted on wheels and faced with corrugated iron sheeting. The sparse interior would include little apart from a stove for cooking and for heating milk for the sickly lambs who would be the shepherd's only companions at such times. His bed was usually no more than a straw bale. Basic as these premises were, it was one up on his poor old grandfather who had nothing but a rude shelter formed by thatching a couple of sheep hurdles. Shepherding was a specialist occupation usually earning a rate above the farm labourers. Their duties included driving the flocks across country to the

Sheep-shearing at Northside Yard, Seagram's Farm 1919/20. Left to right: Silas Pearce,
Harry Meaden, Albert Daniell, Enos Matthews and Harry Marsh.

big sheep fairs and midsummer shearing nearer the village 'when plenty of
light beer was drunk and a lot of leg-pulling went on!'

The beer came from the brewhouse at Imber Court and during
haymaking and harvest time it was taken up to the fields by horse and cart.
On one occasion some gypsies, of whom there were many on the Plain,
were making a nuisance of themselves in the Bell Inn and fighting started. As
there was no full time policeman in the village, Gladys's mother, Kate Dean,
felt she should intervene as the pub was directly opposite Imber Court. She
crossed to the bar where the row was going on and told the landlord not to
sell any more beer. However, as he was lying helpless on the floor she felt it
was her duty as the unofficial 'lady of the manor' to do something. Gladys
was sent off on her bicycle to fetch the special constable from the far side
of the village. Apparently he was not at all enthusiastic about the idea of
confronting pugnacious gypsies and was mightily relieved on arrival to find
the fracas at an end.

Thomas Carter's family had lived for generations in the village and
he grew up among sheep admiring the shepherd's great skill in dealing with

Thomas Carter, gardener and groom of the Deans at Imber Court for 15 years, taught himself to play a cello made by his great grandfather. It had previously been used at Sunday morning services held by shepherds on the downs above Imber.

them. 'They used to love their sheep and wouldn't see a sheep or lamb hurt on any account.' His father James was parish clerk as well as gardener and groom at the vicarage, and used to send his son to ring the eight o'clock bell for the early Sunday morning service, warning him not to get the bell rope looped around his neck. (This was no idle warning as Frank Daniels was almost hanged in the church belfry in 1902 when the bells were being rung. The rope was looped around his neck as a careless prank and he was lifted aloft!)

But shepherding was not the only skill learned by Thomas Carter in his youth. Having received fortnightly music lessons from the vicar, he was keen to progress further. At home he taught himself to play a cello which his great grandfather had made many years previously. It had been used in earlier years in one of the most picturesque of ancient Wiltshire customs: the Sunday morning service held by the shepherds on the downs above Imber. Silently Thomas practised fingering on a cut-out cardboard replica of the cello's finger board. At fourteen he competed successfully against his older brothers, his father having promised that the best performer should have it. Later he joined a small ensemble consisting of four violins (one played by the vicar's son), a flageolet and his cello. They played at the vicarage and occasionally gave small concerts. Thomas worked for two years as a shepherd before becoming groom and gardener to the Dean family . He remained with the family at Imber Court for fifteen years then sought employment elsewhere. The cello remained as a treasured family possession.

By 1901 Imber had been reduced to a small commercial base of little more than one pub, a blacksmith's forge, a carpenter's shop, Harry Meaden's boot and shoe business, a bakery and grocery combined and Mrs Staples general provisions shop in the Barracks. One craft most notable in its decline was that of the dewpond makers who had been associated with the village for generations. The Revd Edgar Glanfield, vicar of Imber 1917-24, recorded the activities of four remarkable men still living at that time and worthy examples of the benefits of an active physical life. Charles White aged 81, Joel Cruse aged 79, Jabez Earley and Daniel Pearce both nearly 80 were all members of this trade. Until around 1912 they had carried on their regular and hereditary craft. Joel Cruse was the youngest of seven children and by the age of ten the boys were helping

Dewpond Making. This was an ancient craft associated with Imber. In this picture Charles White, the leader, is shown on the right with his brother Robert thought to be shown on the left. In between are Jabez Earley and William Carter.

their father John with the trade, some having left school as early as seven in order to do so. John junior and Henry later left the trade to make their own successful careers in the police force.

Starting in September, the dewpond makers toured the country for six to seven months making in sequence from six to fifteen ponds according to size in a season of winter and spring. In the drier summer months they supplemented their income by farm work or by laying floors and constructing mud walls made from flint, chalk and chopped straw. With three assistants at 18 shillings (£0.90) a week, a dewpond maker would take about four weeks to construct a pond 22 yards square which would support a flock of around 400 sheep. Providing all his own tools and appliances he would charge about £40 for the work.

A dewpond is a shallow man-made hollow, roughly eight feet deep, with an impervious bottom made from consolidated layers of clay and straw set hard with a layer of lime. It is found on chalk downland and other high and dry places where there is no adequate supply of water. It is fed mainly by rain water and thus misnamed for dew would play little part. A 'sheep pond', as shown on the Andrews and Dury's map of Wiltshire 1773, would be a better description. They were of particular value on Salisbury Plain with its high downland sustaining vast flocks of sheep. A surrounding wooden or iron fence was usually erected which enabled the sheep to gain entrance but which kept out larger animals whose hoofs would damage the bed.

Charles White, who had a special commission with the Ecclesiastical Commissioners, ran the business with Joel Cruse. Dan Pearce worked with them and, later, Jabez Earley who was related to Joel Cruse by marriage and fathered nine children at Imber. They pushed their equipment in a wheelbarrow, reputedly as far as Kent, returning home at weekends. On one occasion while digging a dewpond on Chapel Down by the Imber windmill, they uncovered a mass grave, possibly the site of an ancient battle. It was filled in and the pond re-dug on an adjoining pitch. Great Wood Pond by Wadman's Copse was also constructed by them as well as the last pond to be made at Winchester.

The work of dewpond makers involved technical skill and much hard physical labour. The decrease in importance of sheep, increasing costs and the development of the wind-driven water pump extracting water from wells, were the main factors in their decline by the end of the 19th century. Nor was the ensuing generation so enthusiastic about doing this work which was so arduous and poorly paid. The last dewpond in Wiltshire is believed to have been made in 1938 by the Smith family of West Lavington.

Jabez Earley, a dew-pond maker, shown at his home in France Buildings. Jabez married Ann Cruse who was the sister of Joel another prominent dewpond maker. Jabez and Ann had nine children all born at Imber.

Accounts of Imber life in the early 20th century abound in old newspapers and the recorded memories of its elderly inhabitants. Beatrice Pearce, for example, married to one of Jabez Earley's sons, Archibald, was the daughter of a shepherd working for the Dean family. As a girl in the village she worked for a baker, Jane Daniel, who taught her the art of bread and cake making. The bakery, presumably the one later run by Mr Webb, lay just west of the Bell Inn. During the winter men would cut out and tie up gorse for heating the bread oven for one shilling a day. Beatrice's mother had a reputation in the village as a good needlewoman making smocks or 'bag-shalleys' for the agricultural labourers. (Another noted needlewoman was Eva Goddard who later won the Gold Star for an embroidery she

Henry Cruse was born at Imber in 1840. He joined the Wilts Constabulary in 1866 and served for 30 years in stations right across the county. When he died in 1935, aged 95, he was believed to be the oldest police pensioner in Great Britain. His brother John had earlier joined the Somerset Constabulary and was stationed at Martock.

made for St Paul's Cathedral). Part of Beatrice's work at the bakery was to push the bread truck through the village to make deliveries. In old age she remembered visits to the windmill at that time run by the landlord of the Bell, Thomas Goddard.

Vivid among her recollections was the engagement of Willie Dean from Imber Court to May Notley around 1900. There was a big party to celebrate the event on Shrub Down. Emanuel ('Buffey') Meaden was the local carrier at that time – Devizes on Thursdays, Warminster on Saturdays. He had been commissioned to bring up the refreshments. On his return later the wagon tipped over by Stocks Arch at the bottom of Church Street scattering his cargo of empties all over the road. Beatrice recalled her childhood trips with Buffey along the hot, dusty track to Warminster when the children had to jump from the wagon and help push it up the hills. The journey cost a shilling and took about two hours. Along the cart track to Gore Cross, the journey was cheaper if you travelled on the milk carts which carried churns of milk and other dairy produce from the farms to Lavington Railway Station each day. Later Beatrice worked as a nursemaid for the Hooper family at Maddington, bringing her charges over each Christmas to stay with their grandfather William Pearce Hooper at Brown's Farm.

The Wedding of Dan Nash and Annie Pearce around the time of the First World War. Back row left to right: Nelson Carter and his sister Fanny Carter, Walter Coleman, Dan Nash, Annie Pearce, her brother Harry, and Kate Wyatt half sister to the bride (the man at the end is not recorded). Front row: May Goddard, Ella Meaden, Percy Wyatt, Lizzie Goddard, Sidney Pearce with John Wyatt, Kate's son, on his lap.

One person to suffer from the Imber weather and to experience the kindness of its village folk was Frank Maidment. Frank was the sub-postmaster at Chitterne, a position he subsidised by the sale of groceries and provisions at his shop in the Shrewton road. He was also the minister of the chapel next door and in 1891 was invited to take a service at Imber. He must have made a good impression for in 1907, following the death of Joseph Goddard, he was invited by the elders to take an oversight of the Imber chapel. This he accepted, preaching regularly to the small community of Baptists there for the next 36 years until the evacuation. His later memoirs show him to have performed these duties with great diligence and fortitude, having buried in his time over 100 people in the little graveyard.

On one occasion, while cycling from Chitterne to take a service, he found the flood water had reached above pedal height. 'I was obliged to go into a widow's house, took off my socks, tipped the water out of my boots and left my socks to dry, and had my wet boots to stand and preach in.' Some time later there was a further misfortune:

> A stone cut the tyre of my bike almost off. Two young men near the chapel said, 'Got a puncture there?' I said, 'Yes'. 'Let us have it,' (they didn't go to the chapel), 'we will repair it.' After the service it was against the chapel ready, so I called to pay. They said, 'After all you do for our people, coming all weathers for funerals, weddings and services free, no nothing, only a pleasure to do anything for you.'

Bertha Meaden, like so many, worked in domestic service after leaving the village. When celebrating her 90th birthday she gave an interview to the *Warminster Journal* recalling Imber's simple pleasures and the hard working character of the people. The Meadens were one of the oldest of the village families going back many generations. Her mother was a member of the Daniel family and her father Harry one of the village's more colourful characters. By trade a village shoemaker, he also worked as a sheep-shearer when the need arose, kept bees and, as noted earlier, was a lay preacher in the Baptist fraternity. In order to preach the Gospel he would walk miles to services, even as far as Devizes.

Bertha left school at ten and was barely thirteen when she started work as a nursemaid. She was the eldest of six children (two others died in childhood) including one boy, Stephen, who was apprenticed to the blacksmith's trade with Albie Nash and later continued with his own business at Salisbury. Harry, her father, made pairs of stout, hardwearing boots for twelve shillings (£0.60):

> They were fashioned from real leather and fitted with strong iron tips for long wear. Customers sometimes popped into his workshop, helped themselves to nails and a hammer and did their own minor repairs! [I] remember one satisfied person coming in and saying 'Yur, Henry. I've bin wurring thic yur pair o' boots vur vower years or more. An' wass think? I've nivver 'ad nothin' done to um. Dost thee reckon tiz time vur zum repairs?'

Bertha's uncle, Buffy Meaden, was later to be followed as village carrier by Frank Wyatt whose family lived at the Dring, the westernmost part of the village. Later a bus was provided running from Warminster to Devizes and back the same day. It brought Imber into closer touch with other areas bringing friends and relatives, like Gwen Gentry the Meaden's granddaughter, to visit. It also brought stock for the Post Office, shop and pub. Water came from the numerous wells in the area and most houses had their own detached 'privy' kept in good order by its owner and providing nourishment for the allotments situated north of the main street. When a new seat for a privy was required, a village carpenter was called for. He would make the owner sit on the wood whilst he drew around his bottom to ensure the right size! Agricultural wages at the turn of the 20th century at Imber were nine shillings (£0.45) a week although shepherds were paid rather more. This was the sole income to feed and clothe large families often as many as ten.

Right: Charlotte and Henry (Harry) Meaden. This picture was taken in 1908 on the downs during the 'Anniversary Trial', presumably a sheep dog competition. Charlotte had been a member of the Daniels family before her marriage. Harry was a shepherd, shoemaker and a deacon at the Imber Baptist Chapel. They had eight children, five of whom survived to adulthood including Bertha Knight of Warminster who died in 1969 aged 92.

Opposite: Charlotte Meaden the wife of the shepherd and shoemaker Harry Meaden. Charlotte and Harry were both buried in the Baptist graveyard.

Vivid among Bertha Meaden's earliest memories were the visits of travelling showmen. When she was eight some swing boats were erected near her home adjacent to Stocks Arch. Unfortunately they could not have chosen a worse spot. They were straddled across Imber Dock. Due to heavy rain, the road was very soft. The pegs failed to hold and the swings lurched wildly. 'I could see and hear these pegs splitting – then the swing turned us over and threw us into the ditch as it toppled down', recalled Bertha, 'some of the boys and girls on the swinging boats were wearing their Sunday best clothing at the time'.

A Chapel gathering at Imber. The cart would suggest the congregation is going on some sort of outing. This picture, taken early in the 20th century, shows the chapel to have been a flourishing concern and includes a fair representation of the village community. Members of the Meaden, Wyatt, Potter, Marsh and Nash families are among those shown. The bearded man to the left of the middle row is Harry Meaden the shoemaker. The pastor, Frank Maidment from Chitterne is in the centre wearing a boater.

* * *

Exactly when military activities in the Imber area began is not clear but it is likely that manoeuvres of some description were carried on from the end of the 19th century bringing the two into uneasy co-existence. As the potential for training on Salisbury Plain became evident, plans were put in

Ladywell. This small farm lay to the west of Imber near the junction with the Bratton road. Mr A. G. Wright lived there with his wife and children Bernard and Gladys (who died of flu in the 1918-19 epidemic). Beyond the farm lay the rabbit warren.

hand by the government to acquire suitable available sites. The War Office Salisbury Plain Committee (WOSP), convened in 1897, had acquired 40,000 acres of land by 1902, but this was mainly to the east of the Plain. Nevertheless, the easy-going peaceful atmosphere of Imber would have been disturbed . Over the clatter of the farm machinery, the rumbling of passing wagons and the sounds of normal domestic life, other sounds were beginning to intrude. The concussion of distant artillery, thundering hoofs of cavalry horses on the downland and columns of soldiers on exercise disturbed their daily routine. As the situation in Europe deteriorated military activity increased with the build-up to the First World War, a war which was to have a considerable impact upon Imber.

With the outbreak of hostilities in 1914 Salisbury Plain became one of the most important training centres in the country. Despite its remoteness and the appalling winter of 1914-15, tented accommodation began to appear on the downs as the War Office used the area increasingly for intensive training and artillery ranges. The occasional appearance of mysterious mobile metal boxes must have caused astonishment to those who encountered them on the downland tracks. Manufactured at Bratton Iron Works, they were one of the prototypes of the military 'landships' developed from transportable water containers used to water livestock. They were supposedly a top secret project and gave their name to the military tank used for the first time on the Somme in 1916.

In the same year, an artillery school was established on Chapperton Down between Imber and Tilshead extending the range of guns and the area of military activity still further. Great consternation was experienced at Imber Court when an officer arrived to say that troops would have to be billeted there. Forty foot-soldiers and six batmen were housed in the attic, with a major and five other officers in more comfortable accommodation. Gladys Dean and one of the maids provided tea for them before their departure at 6 am each morning.

The vast majority of troops living under canvas fared much worse. The experience of the 2/1st City of London Royal Field Artillery, which arrived in November 1916, was certainly typical of thousands of others forced to live in such fashion. Living in a bell tent in the bleakest area of the Plain to the south of Imber, the author, Dennis Wheatley, recalled the full horror in his book, *Officer and Temporary Gentleman*:

> The days that followed were sheer purgatory. The rain increased until it was continuous. Day after day it poured in torrents while the men, protected only by their mackintosh ground-sheets, laced around their necks, toiled at digging gunpits. Our chaps had never before been called on to live in the open, so our cooks had no experience of using camp ovens. Petrol and sugar was flung on the fires in vain, time after time wind-driven rain put them out. During lulls they managed to boil up kettles for tea but nearly all our food had to be eaten cold. On that desolate plain there was not a house or barn in which anyone could shelter even for a short while. Drenched to the skin, their boots sodden, unwashed and utterly miserable, the men crouched shivering in their bivvies...

No wonder that many developed bronchitis and pneumonia. The infantry suffered worse, two of them dying on the Plain – their bodies carted away in small arms wagons. Out of a total force of 498 troops and 16 officers, 170 men were evacuated because of uncontrollable coughing.

As more and more troops flooded the area Imber folk opened their homes to provide welcome relief to soldiers far from home. At the Court, concerts were arranged in the great barn to improve morale. Gladys Dean sang and played the piano. Everyone was encouraged to take part in doing a turn or singing the patriotic songs of the time with Gladys performing the accompaniment.

Kathleen and Gladys, the daughters of Edward and Kate Dean from Imber Court. They are shown with their dog Peter around 1914. Gladys kept a journal which showed her to have been the main instigator of entertainments for the troops stationed in and around Imber during the First World War.

The warmth of such hospitality is much to the credit of the villagers who found their lives turned upside down. Although the army improved the road through the village, the track from Heytesbury came under regular fire. Shells damaged some of the houses and at times the villagers were virtually prisoners, being allowed out only three times a week to shop at Warminster. The vicar, Charles Watling, wrote:

We daily, and often nightly, suffered from the effects of concussion, our walls buckled, our glass cracked, so that we present to the world a shell shocked village... our population has dwindled, one shop remains and instead of our continuing to be a self-supporting community we have become dependent upon neighbouring villages for our thrice weekly supply of food.

Charles Watling left the village in 1917 and it was his successor, Edgar Glanfield, who in November of the following year recorded in the churchwarden's book the relief at the news of a peace treaty. Soldiers billetted in one of the surrounding farm buildings asked whether they might ring a peal of bells as a thanksgiving and he obligingly held a service for them in the evening. Indeed, the magnificent bells, cast by John Lot of Warminster, had been ringing continuously all day, though only three of them; the others were too cracked to use.

Mrs Mullings of Edington took the bread to Imber on Armistice Day as she had many times before during those difficult years. With Mr Marsh, the baker, they drove two bread carts, he in front with the lighter wagon, she following behind with a heavier covered van. From Bratton to Imber, up the steepest part of the escarpment an extra horse was used for the van. Imber's celebrated home-made wines, parsnip, dandelion and many other varieties, were liberally offered along the way – 'very strong they were and very good'. All day long they were feted. At Imber Court they joined a particularly jolly party. Australian soldiers, unaware of the fatal Spanish flu soon to reduce drastically their numbers, were celebrating their anticipation of a swift return home.

It was nine in the evening before they started their woozy return, Mr Marsh with his chestnut-coloured nag, Jimmy, once more leading the way and Mrs Mullings with Jacky pulling the heavier van. By this late hour the track was difficult to manoeuvre and in the dark a piece of wool from the surrounding sheep blew into Jack's face. The horse took fright. 'I thought that was the end of me' remembered Mrs Mullings. She put on the brake as the horse started to bolt. Fortunately he pulled up on reaching the cart in front and they returned home safely.

In 1920 a war memorial was erected in memory of the three servicemen from Imber who died – Ernest Marsh and Harold Kitley, killed in France, and Arthur Norris who died at Gallipoli. Also mentioned were the others who served in various theatres of war:

The War Memorial shown in its original position along the high street in front of Albert Nash's blacksmith shop on land given by James Hooper from Brown's Farm.

A Bundy, W Carter (wounded), L Carter, N D Carter, W I Carter, P A Daniels, H Daniels, L L Daniels, F J Daniels, H W Daniels, E H Daniels, T L Daniels, J T Dean, H Goddard, W W Grey, A J Grey, R A Kitley (wounded), R W Meaden, W A Pearce (wounded), J V Potter, H Potter, F Palmer, R Tinnams, L P Tinnams, W White

The Revd Edgar Glanfield would have preferred oak memorial tables placed in the church and chapel, but a majority of the villagers wanted a memorial erected in a prominent open space. It was a modest wooden cross; the village could afford no more. They erected it on land given by James Hooper from Brown's Farm outside Albie Nash's smithy. Later, for the 50th anniversary of the village evacuation in 1993, this simple tribute was renovated and erected in St Giles's churchyard beside the track leading to the church.

* * *

As the war ended military activities were scaled down. Mules, sold off by the army in large numbers, became a familiar sight as the village gradually returned to a peacetime routine. They were used for all kinds of transportation including agricultural carts, domestic traps and even for carrying water barrels when Imber Dock dried up during the sultry days of summer. Sydney Dean kept a number of mules at Northside Yard opposite his home at Seagrams but there were always complaints when they escaped and traipsed hungrily along the dusty lanes.

Herding sheep through the village. Six year old Audrey (on the right), and Marion (centre), daughters of Frank Carpenter the road man are shown with other friends in 1928. The sheep, like most on the local farms, are Hampshire Downs.

Cyril Nash, son of the blacksmith, certainly regarded the mules with a jaundiced eye. His deep knowledge of the area found him occasional employment with the local military authorities, locating water, digging drains and seeking out officials who had lost their way on the downs. 'A mule is one of the most difficult things to buy, or breed, or kill' he observed drily to friends in the Bell Inn. 'They never, like donkeys, die a natural death, and they kick in every direction like a cow. The men about here say that they'll stand double the work of a horse of their size, but for my part I wouldn't have one for a gift .'

Mollie Dean (now Mrs Archer-Smith) from Seagram's Farm on a Rudge motorcycle in the yard of Brown's Farm.

Sydney Dean continued to farm the land at Seagram's, Tinker's and Parsonage Farms until the evacuation, but at Imber Court the long residence of Edward Dean was over. After his death in 1910 his son Tom continued to oversee the farm. However, following the army occupation during the war the church commissioners sold the property to the Holloways, a wealthy family from Lavington in 1920. The Holloways had developed a very successful building firm in London and invested their capital in the Lavington Estate when it came up for sale in 1905. During renovations after the purchase Imber Court was dramatically destroyed by fire, believed to have been started by a workman's torch. Harwood Daniels and Nelson Potter, out for a walk, saw the menacing flames through a window and raised the alarm, but facilities for fire-fighting in such a remote area were hopelessly inadequate. Immediate

Harvesting at Imber Court Farm. Edward Dean, who farmed here and at Southdown Farm, died in 1910 after a long tenancy. His son Tom then carried on until he joined the Royal Wilts Yeomanry in August 1914. Tom's uncle Joseph then took over the management until the Holloways purchased the estate in 1920.

reconstruction took place and the Court became the home of a retired army major, Robert Whistler, who managed the estate for the Holloways. Among the modern facilities provided in the restored mansion was a generator, a rare luxury as mains electrictiy never reached the village.

Among the finest recollections of Imber life in the first half of the 20th century are those written by Percy (Jack) Pye, a retired policeman, and although tinged with feelings of nostalgia, they nevertheless ring true. Percy's uncle, Albert Nash, was one of the most respected members of the village community throughout the period. Having taken over the blacksmith's business from his Uncle William, Albie had continued to work from the forge in Front Street, part of the main Warminster to Gore Cross road.

A mainstay of the village economy, Albie Nash's tasks included shoeing the farm horses, repairing farm machinery and keeping the bicycles of the village in working order. He was known for miles around as an excellent farrier winning many prizes at agricultural shows. A favourite drink, especially at Christmas, was home-made mead made from the honey obtained from bees which the villagers kept either in inverted boxes or straw-plaited skips. Albie kept several of these hives, obtaining the honey by burning a sulphur candle under the skip.

Tom Dean outside his home Imber Court around 1914. Tom was the only son of Edward Dean and would have expected to continue farming there after his service in the First World War. However, the Court was sold by the Ecclesiastical Commissioners and Tom moved away from Imber to find employment elsewhere, thus ending the long Dean tenancy of Imber Court.

Imber Court, 1920, following its restoration by the Holloways.

Henry Holloway (later knighted), Stella and Ernest Holloway at the rear of Imber Court following its restoration. The Holloways developed a very successful building firm in London and purchased the Court in 1920.

The forge was a constant source of wonder to Percy who lived in Westbury and holidayed on every occasion at Imber. His mother was Albie's younger sister who had been born there in the 1880s at one of the isolated farms on Imber Down where their father worked as a shepherd. Like so many, he was dedicated to his flock, tending them in all weathers by day and night. Percy's grandmother would place lighted candles in the bedroom windows during dark nights to provide homing beacons for her husband as it was so easy to get lost. On one sad occasion a young boy had gone across the downs to help his father with the sheep. It began to snow heavily. The boy became lost and could not find his father. Some days later his body was discovered beside a rick near a plantation of beech trees between Imber and Gore Cross.

Inevitably, Percy's mother had left the village to seek work elsewhere and found it at the Bath Arms, Warminster. On Sunday afternoons, however, in the company of several other young Imber girls, she returned briefly to the home she still yearned for, travelling in a hired wagonette. When Percy was only a few months old, his parents took him to spend Christmas with the Nash's. One night, while his father and Albie were visiting the Bell Inn, the sky to the north became illuminated in a strange fashion:

> The lights were bright and coloured, and my mother and aunt became frightened, feeling sure that the end of the world had come. They gathered the children together and sat under the table, praying to the Lord to preserve them. It was, of course, a rare sighting of the Northern Lights (Aurora Borealis) and it appears that all the villagers who saw this spectacle were similarly scared.

During his boyhood the best times for Percy were the long, dusty days of an Imber summer when he would spend his holidays with the Nash's suitably indulged and able to enjoy village life to the full:

The Blacksmith's Shop. Albert Nash, the last smithy, is shown with 'Janet', a favourite horse belonging to Capt Arthur Williams.

I often, in these present days of hustle and bustle, think of the quiet and peacefulness which existed in this remote village, miles from anywhere. The days were long and, to me, seemed never ending. We were up with the lark and down at the blacksmith's shop where my uncle would shoe possibly half a dozen horses before going to breakfast. Breakfast consisted of bacon (home produced and home cured) and eggs, finishing off with bread and my Aunt Martha's home-made jam. How I remember the mid-day meals of roast rabbit or rabbit stew, with fresh garden vegetables, rice pudding and stewed apple. The best rabbits are those which live on chalk land, my uncle used to say, and I still hear it said in this day and age.

The mornings were usually spent, if fine, by following the binder in the corn field and chasing rabbits which ran out of the corn as it was being cut. It was nothing unusual to see a fox run out as well as the rabbits. It was esteemed a very great favour if you were allowed to ride on the back of the trace horse which was used to assist in pulling the binder on hilly ground. It was the usual custom, weather being suitable, to gather the sheaves of corn during the afternoons and evenings. We were then allowed to lead the horses along the

The Blacksmith's Shop – bonding a wheel. From left to right are shown: Harry Marsh, Dollie Coleman (or Flossie Nash), Billie Burgess, Edward Marsh, Edward Pearce, Frank Carpenter and Albert Nash the blacksmith.

Threshing with a steam engine before the First World War. This picture was taken at Northside Yard belonging to Seagram's Farm where Sydney Dean was the farmer. On the threshing machine at the rear is Harry Marsh with his son Ernest who was killed in the First World War. Left to right in front are: Billie Burgess, Sydney Dean, William Pearce, John Marsh and Silas Pearce.

rows of 'stooks' (stacks) of cornsheaves, stopping at each stook for the loaders to pitch the sheaves on to the wagon. In the middle of the afternoon we had to run back home to collect our tea and that of the farm workers and take it to the corn field. Tea consisted of thick slices of bread with lashings of butter and home-made jam, followed by home-made cake washed down with quite warm tea from a bottle which was contained in one or more woollen socks to conserve heat. Everyone saved a drop of tea to slake the throat during the evening. Work kept on until darkness began to fall, when the horses were unharnessed from the wagons and set off for home, man and boy alike riding on the broad sweaty backs of the horses. Everyone was ready for supper – bread and cheese with home-grown beetroot, cooked and sliced in vinegar and flavoured with sliced onion, lettuce and tomatoes grown in a greenhouse erected from a number of old windows nailed together.

But the echoes of war were never far away. The agricultural depression of the Twenties and Thirties was deeply felt at Imber as elsewhere. Grain prices reached their lowest ebb and the prices of wool and mutton fared little better. Cattle were tried instead of sheep with only marginal success. Cattle were not natural to the downs, said the old folk, 'we drink only goats' milk.' Imber's remoteness from the markets and poor weather made large-scale vegetable cultivation unsuitable. Not surprisingly, the village population continued its long decline and land prices reached rock bottom. The vacuum was filled by the army's desire to acquire more land. As the European political situation became less stable Salisbury Plain again became a focus for increasing military requirements. Mechanical and armoured warfare in particular meant more land was needed for training and the Plain with its few natural obstacles was ideal. In the centre of this new area lay Imber.

Church outing to Bournemouth 1922 or 23. In the back row are A. Cruse, Mrs H. Nash, Miss A. Cruse, Miss F. Carpenter, G. Rebbeck and E. Daniels. In the front are Frank Carpenter, S. Matthews, Cyril Nash, H. Nash, E. Greening, F. Pearce, D. Wyatt and Stuart Carter.

In 1927 the War Office concentrated its efforts to obtain further territory to the west of the Devizes Road from Shrewton to West Lavington. Austin Underwood, who was to play a major part in Imber's fight for survival after the war, was withering in his description of the army's efforts to woo the local farmers:

Hostility would not be a term I would apply to the farmers of Imber carrying the negative attitude that it does. 'Prickly' is the word. Prickly they certainly were, almost superstitiously jealous of their birthright. Ambassadors to the Bell Inn, after their pint at the bar and listening to the opinions of the farmers, returned to the War Office and advised them to play it ca'canny with the farmers of Imber . . .

The years of agricultural depression forced many a small farmer to surrender. Down at the Bell the spider's promises were often the subject of lively discussion and at odd moments a War Office ambassador would stop off for a drink and never miss a chance to count the blessings for those who would only step into the parlour.

The large type was euphoric, the small type more sinister. Four words were written – 'The right of presumption' that summed up the position of farmers who had sold their birthright. It could, and it did, involve the right to take away, with hardly any notice their former land and agricultural possessions. To those who were sub-tenants, a term of which the sub-tenant hardly knew the significance, like that grand old blacksmith, Albert Nash, compensation on resumption would be, and was – nil. So with a heavy heart one by one the farmers succumbed and with their surrender and on their eviction those farmworkers who were sub-tenants would be left high and dry.

The tenancy agreements offered to the Imber farmers varied but was generally considered quite reasonable. The Hoopers at Brown's Farm, for example, were offered £20 an acre. Stock-proof fencing, gates and other maintenance work were also financed by taxpayers' money. The land was divided into two sections: Schedule I and Schedule III. Schedule I land was rented at ten shillings (£0.50) an acre per annum to the farmer and compensation given for any damage done by the army. Schedule III land was rented at two shillings and sixpence (£0.12½) per acre but with no compensation in the event of damage. As a general rule areas under crops were Schedule I and those for sheep and cattle, which could be moved before a military exercise, were Schedule III.

Such an arrangement was received with grudging satisfaction. The land – usually rented back to the previous owner at a rate comparable to normal market rates – was on a yearly basis and during the inter-war years it was assumed that the lease would be renewed automatically. Normally the army only required it for the two-week annual exercises after the harvest. Damage was slight and usually involved little more than repairs to damaged

The Wylye Valley Hunt causes some excitement as it passes through Imber before the
Second World War.

fences. Under such relatively favourable terms and with the pressure of low
farm prices it is not surprising that between 1928-32 all the Imber farmers
sold up. The bargaining was done individually, and although all sales were
voluntary, rumours persisted at the time that a refusal to sell might well lead
to a lower compulsory price being imposed later.

By 1932, therefore, with a naïve unawareness of events to come, the
farmers had relinquished the whole of the village to the War Department
with the exception of the chapel, the Bell Inn and the property (the church,
vicarage and school) under the control of the church commissioners. War
Office papers at Kew show that a policy to evacuate all cottages in the
village was considered even at this date though reversed in 1934. One
local at the Bell, armed apparently with inside information, was reported to
have remarked that the War Office had plans to use Imber for experimental
shelling. 'Tis only the corpses in the churchyard that have saved the village
from being blown to pieces,' said the bar room sage. 'The church will not
let them remove or damage the bodies!'

James and Patrick McEvoy, one an aspiring writer, the other an artist, toured the area at this time. With the aid of a small tent and a horse and trap, they were hoping to rent a piece of land on which to build a small cabin and work in solitude. Their description gives us an impression of the village in those final years before the Second World War led to its demise:

> The farms and cottages in Imber are built of red brick reinforced with tarred oak beams. On one side of the road is a kind of dyke or stream, spanned at intervals by wooden and stone bridges. The stream, however, was quite dry and only two wells out of twenty were in use in the village. Most of the cottages are set back about 30 yards from the road and between the ends of their gardens and the pavement runs a wall, made of mud, rubble, lime and straw and covered on top with a narrow thatch.

In 1938 the army demolished a number of these mud-walled cottages lying along the High street and re-housed the occupants in new homes built

Imber School between the wars. (Original photograph lent by Mrs Gladys Mitchell). Back row: Harold Carter, Ron Wyatt, Reg Chapman, William White, Stephen Chapman and Len Potter. Second row: Miss Burgess (from Westbury), Hilda Rebbeck, Betty Pearce, Myra Pearce, (front) Win Rebbeck, Phyllis Daniels, (front) Maggie Carter, Stella Chapman and a member of the White family. Front row: Cyril Nash, Frank Rebbeck, Violet Potter, Ray Wyatt, Violet Rebbeck, Mary Pearce, ? White, Dorothy Rebbeck and Douglas Chapman.

by Plumber and Hockey of Radstock. Derrick Mitchell, grandson of Albert Nash, was one of the new tenants and recalls them with little enthusiasm. 'The houses were built to a budget with outside bucket lavatories and with crude hardcore paths. There was a barbed wire fence around them which made life very difficult' Nevertheless, there was hot and cold running water – and a bath – a luxury for Imber folk!'

But the problems of water for the village persisted. Imber Dock – dry in summer and producing excessive floods through the long winter months – remained a constant source of worry. The *Warminster Gazette* reported one particularly anxious period in 1934 when an acute water shortage affected the village over a long period of time. For weeks the population had only two sources of supply: a well belonging to Major Whistler at Imber Court, and another to Sydney Dean. When these dried out, the villagers were reduced to catching every possible drop of rainwater in a desperate attempt to carry them through. Asked whether the War Office were preparing a scheme to give the village a constant supply, the weary response was, 'The War Office have had the matter in hand for some time but nothing appears to be done.'

During the last winter before war again broke out snow blocked all the entrance roads. Once more floods cut off the village by road and telephone. One valiant journalist, fired with enthusiasm and youthful zeal, made an unsuccessful attempt to get there. He was met by a farm labourer, a philosopher of the Imber soil, who accepted his lot with resignation and could imagine no other existence:

> Luckily I met no cars coming down and up and up I climbed until the heights alongside Battlesbury and overlooking the lovely downland in all directions came into view. I halted and had a glance back at Warminster in the fear that this trip into the 'arctic' might mean disaster.
>
> Warminster Camp was cloaked in snow and beyond it Cop Heap wore a glorious mantle of white. The hills and vales had new suits on. Once more Imber was the objective. Onwards through the single track and then the car ploughed its way downwards after passing the 'Clump', a spot where I have often picked mushrooms. Down the slope I made a perilous descent to Ladywell Crossroads. On the way I saw two black objects coming towards me like tortoises creeping towards civilisation. They were cars. Later I found one had been under a drift for five days and had just been rescued.

IMBER
CORONATION CELEBRATIONS
AT IMBER COURT.

Coronation of
George VI, May 12
1937 – details on
the booklet cover.

Stewards:

Rev. W. Walser   Charles Hooper, Esq.

Capt. A. C. Williams   Sidney G. Dean, Esq.

Judges:

Rev. W. Walser   S. G. Dean, Esq.

Captain A. C. Williams

Starter:

Peter Whistler

Clerk of Course and Handicapper:

Major R. Whistler

Committee:

F. Carpenter   F. Mitchell

A. Goddard   E. Matthews

and all I.C.C. Members.

OFFICIAL SPORTS PROGRAMME - PRICE 6d.

On the flat, a mile from Imber, water was bubbling out of the surface of the downs. But I reached Imber, and there saw a typical farmhand watching the rising torrent. Yes, I was unlucky . . snowed up for nearly a week and then invaded by floods. But the Imberonian – that's a new word – was quite calm in this sea of trouble. He told me that if I wanted to reach anywhere, I must turn back, as some thirty cars and other vehicles were in the fields snowed under. The drivers had tried the fields in a last effort to break through the barrier of snow.

The 'local' said: 'Life in Imber is not what it used to be. The War Office bin and cum and spoiled it all. We had three big farms here, and used to grow the best corn in England. But now the War Office have bought the lot. They be knocking down our cottages and the place will never be wat it was.' I said 'but surely you would prefer to live somewhere better than Imber, which has to face floods and snow, and has none of the comforts of the outside world.' The Imber man looked at me sternly and said, 'There waddon no place better than Imber before they started knocking it about, and there idden a better place today.'

By this time the flood waters were washing over their boots and the Warminster journalist, like the stranger from Porlock, returned from whence he came.

Bernie Wright (1902-1980) is shown on a Triumph motorbike outside the Post Office. On the 27 November 1943, he married Phyllis Daniels. It was the last wedding to be celebrated at St Giles Church before the evacuation closed the village.

5 Forty-Seven Days

What we have seen from our glimpses into the life of Imber indicates a small, remote community on Salisbury Plain, independent, hardworking in character and enjoying simple pleasures. Harold Massingham, an early-20th century biographer and nature writer, regarded Imber as one of the loveliest and loneliest places in the world referring to its isolation in fanciful terms: 'a little lightship sailing the Wiltshire Downs'. Tramps, it was said, rarely visited; they could not stand the loneliness. Even gypsies, travelling through in familial groups, their gaily-decorated caravans covered in white chalk dust, rarely stopped long except in mushroom season. Few villagers had seen a film or travelled by train. (There was, however, during the interwar years a weekly bus linking Warminster with Devizes via Imber so a journey could be made to either town and back within the day). The annual outing to one of the nearer seaside resorts, such as Weston-super-Mare, was the highlight of the year. A successful cricket team played on the Barley Ground throughout the season and The Bell Inn, incorporating a small shop at the back for groceries and confectionery, provided a cheerful focus for social gatherings. Tennis parties were a popular feature at all the main farmhouses, Seagram's, Brown's, Tinker's and Imber Court. Mollie Archer-Smith, daughter of Sydney and Gladys Dean from Seagram's Farm, recalled 72 couples at their last event. Shooting parties of ten or twelve guns continued to be a popular pursuit among this fraternity followed by card playing in the evenings. 'Imber was a hive of social activity,' recalled Betty Hooper from Cornbury Farm. 'There were grand dances, too, which would end with breakfast at 4 am. Then we'd do the milking still in our tails and waistcoats!'

Building a corn rick for Major Robert Whistler. Whistler was the farm manager for Henry Holloway and lived with his family at Imber Court. One man on the rick is Fred Daniels, another is Jack Potter.

Not only the character of the village, but the character of its inhabitants, too, was determined largely by its isolation. Imber's separateness had made it more self-supporting than many other places, its past commercial activities ranging from cordwainer and windmiller to dewpond maker. Its inhabitants, despite infrequent contact with doctors and hospitals, were generally healthy and long-lived. Almost all accounts of village life indicate that its long population decline from a high point of 440 in 1851 to around 150 in 1939, was caused – not by any dissatisfaction with the village - but by the over-riding need to find employment.

One visitor to the village in those last peacetime years described Imber as a village of neglect and decay. 'The place looked desolate, miserable and almost dead . . . There is very little apart perhaps from the church, that can be called picturesque, much less beautiful'. Monica Hutchings, however, making the first of her many visits while a young girl at school in Warminster, loved the peace and serenity of the place set among the high, rolling tableland of the Plain. On her second visit in 1939 she was even more effusive:

The village bloomed more than ever among the bare downs. Old cottages had been reconditioned and new ones built. All was trim neat and well cared for. The new cottages impressed me as being superior to the usual Council house. They were set well back from the road, were of pleasing design and had substantial gardens.

Arthur Mee, researching for his Wiltshire volume in 'The King's England' series, gave us perhaps the last glimpse of the 13th-century St Giles's Church as a living entity admiring the impressive tombs of what he took to be crusaders, surmounted by their impressive chain-mailed and cross-legged effigies:

It is an attractive Church in which the old crusaders lie. Its tower, like the porch and its charming doorway, is 500 years old. On its walls inside are the fading figures of the table of changes for the ringers, painted by a 17th century hand. A rough Jacobean screen shuts the ringers off from the nave. The great bowl of the Norman font, greeting us as we come in, has a band of herringbone round the top and a wooden cover of the 17th century. From the same time come most of the carved pews, the simply decorated pulpit, the charmingly carved stalls in the chancel, and three chairs by the altar. The Nave has ancient frescoes fading on the walls and an old wagon roof in which we notice a boss carved with a mitred Churchman. There are some fragments

Children in front of the vicarage gate 1941/2. Back row left to right: Horace Pearce, Doreen Mitchell, Alec Potter, Melba Potter and Reggie Weller. Seated: June Wyatt, Ida Skidmore (from Bristol), Edward Carter, Jean Wyatt and an evacuee. Front row: an evacuee (probably William Meaden), Lionel Daniels and Desmond Lacy.

of old glass, one piece with a small head of Christ, and below this window when we called were two old coffin stools by a Jacobean altar.

War returned to Imber with no dramatic suddenness, but with an ever-increasing intensity of military activity enveloping the whole area. Monica Hutchings had noticed that the romantic white tents of Warminster Camp had been replaced by an ugly rash of red brick barracks and living quarters spread across the downs. The Plain once again assumed vital importance. Exercises with live ammunition made the risk of civilian casualties, particularly in the Imber area, a worrying possibility. But the villagers reacted stoically – all that is who had not departed on war duties. Food production was increased and prisoners-of-war sent to help with the harvest. In 1940, Jack Walker, a soldier with the 48th Tank Regiment stationed on the Plain, fell in love with Daisy, a young girl from the village. Wedding banns were read at St Giles's and the ceremony went ahead in due course even though Jack was 5s. (£0.25) short of the 7s. 6d. (£0.37½) required for the licence fee! A batch of evacuees arrived. 'They came on a Saturday night much to our surprise,' remembers Derrick Mitchell. 'My grandparents had three of them but most went back to London after six months.'

A fancy dress group around the beginning of the Second World War. Back row left to right: Kathie Jenkins, Horace Potter, Jack Potter, Marion Carpenter, Ken Mitchell, Derek Mitchell. Front row: Two Jenkins boys, Melba Potter, Ken Pearce, Ron Daniels, Elsie Ayres and Doreen Mitchell. Alec Potter is the child in front.

A company of the Home Guard was commanded by Capt Williams from Brown's Farm, but the nearest A.R.P. warden was Norris Hooper from Cornbury. The detachment was based at Lavington and their only equipment between twelve men was one pair of wellington boots, size 9, and one tin hat. Norris had the hat as he had to stop the traffic at Gores Cross and needed some sign of authority! Air attack by enemy aircraft was inevitable in an area so thickly inhabited by military training activity and the village was bombed several times with little harm caused. On 17 September 1940, a badly shot-up Junkers 88 with two crew aboard, one dead and the other injured, flew low over the village, circled it and crash-landed nearby.

Capt Arthur Williams from Brown's Farm with the family dogs. He was married to Hilda, sister of Charlie Hooper, who was living at this time at another Hooper farm at Deptford. Arthur Williams had served on the gunnery ranges at Imber during the First World War.

It was incendiary bombs, commonly known as 'Molotov cocktails', that caused the greatest potential danger during these raids. Norris and Betty Hooper were married in 1933 and went to live at Cornbury Farm on the eastern downland from Imber close to Gore Cross. It had just come back into Hooper tenancy and here they farmed over a thousand acres plus additional grazing land necessary for the two flocks of sheep. One evening in 1941 a card party was held in their farmhouse following a shoot. It ended about midnight and the cars departed down the Cornbury road in a convoy – night driving being very difficult with wartime restrictions limiting the amount of light each car could use. Whether it was the car lights that were detected or the R.A.F. air strip at nearby New Zealand Farm, an air attack took place. Betty recalls hearing a sound like corrugated tin falling from the sky, the ominous sound of incendiary bombs dropping on Imber. Fred Daniels had one at his back door. Arthur Goddard one on his motor bike shed. Hooper's Yard was the worst hit with bombs falling in the tractor sheds. The Deans at Seagram Farm also had one close to the farm with others falling in the stockyard. Fortunately, however, most fell on Chitterne Hill.

Norris Hooper had remained at home listening apprehensively to the thump of the bombs. When they did not explode, his Air Raid Warden training warned him they were delayed action bombs. Canadian troops were encamped along the Imber road. They had recently returned from Dunkirk dressed in little more than rags. They were weaponless, but had been issued with pickaxe handles and were in a very vulnerable position. Norris went up to inform them of the possible danger. Many were sleeping in slit trenches and had heard nothing. However the following morning delayed action bombs went off, one in the Canadian camp and another in Charlie Hooper's sheepfold near Browns Farm, showering chalk over the indignant shepherd as he was pitching the fold.

In the following spring, Norris took his thrashing machine from Cornbury to Imber to thrash some oats for his cousin Charlie at Browns Farm. They had been stored in the big barn since the previous harvest. The thrashing machine was pulled through the large doors into the barn so that the oat sheaves could be fed directly into the machine. This was done, and when the men climbed up on to the sheaves they found an incendiary bomb which had fallen through the thatched roof and, fortunately, not ignited. At nearby Seagram's Farm, Molly Dean, serving with the First Aid Nursing Yeomanry (FANYS), was home on leave. Hearing a commotion, she ran downstairs in her pyjamas. Grabbing a tin hat, she rushed out of the back door in the process of which she tripped over another incendiary bomb that had also remained inactive! Mrs Carter, the postmistress, remarked how difficult it was to deal with these burning bombs with the stirrup pumps supplied by the Ministry of Defence. As soon as one was doused and another was being dealt with, the previous one would start burning all over again! It was truly amazing that there were no casualties and so little damage.

But these were small, local affairs to be expected by any town or village situated within a vital industrial or military area in times of war. To be exposed to allied fire power was a much more worrying prospect. The War Department had scheduled a safety zone of 1,000 yards around Imber inside which no shelling was to take place, but there was also the problem of access. As Ralph Whitlock put it, 'not only had the village to be avoided during military exercises on the Plain but the long, exposed roads over the downs had to be kept open, for Imber's use and for Imber's alone'. Situated so conveniently close to the strategic ports of Southampton, London and Bristol, Salisbury Plain was the only suitable large-scale site for miles; the pressure for additional land there was immense. Imber lay in the middle of an area for practising with long-range guns. Consideration was also given to the possibility that the area might be used for tank training in place of artillery. With continuing development in the size, range and sophistication of armoured weaponry, the War Office would have been pleased to remove this obstruction by evacuating the village much earlier given a satisfactory opportunity.

Despite further de-population by service requirements, Imber continued with a surprising degree of normality. Reg Meaden and Derrick Mitchell were two of a declining number of young people still trying to complete their education. Reg was the grandson of William and Annie Meaden who lived in one of two cottages next to the Barley Field. William was a carter for Major Whistler at Imber Court Farm and his son, Reginald William Meaden, had moved from the village in 1917 to join the Royal Marines serving for 29 years. He lived at Plymouth but, as he was often serving in other theatres of military activity, his family would return to Imber each summer to spend long holidays there. When their Plymouth home was destroyed by bombs early in the war they were able to find accommodation at Church Cottage near the entrance to St Giles's Church. The cottage was cleaned out and they lived there on the understanding that they would keep the church clean – a task which involved fumigating the tower, thus reducing the intrusion by hundreds of bats.

Derrick Mitchell was born at Imber in 1928 in the area off the High Street known as the Barracks. His mother, Gladys, was a daughter of the blacksmith, Albert Nash:

> My mother went into service at Bishopstone when Freddy Dean from Tinker's Farm moved there. After my parents married they returned to Imber where father was gardener at the Vicarage. About 1940 he went to work at Imber Court Farm for Major Whistler and continued there until the evacuation. In 1938, we moved from the Barracks to one of the new houses.
>
> The military activity was beginning to build up during the thirties, but to me, as a young boy, it was all a bit of excitement. I went to school in Imber when there were only about 12-15 pupils left. At eleven I was transferred to Samborne School in Warminster travelling with others in Percy Hicks' car. There was, in fact, no attempt to make life difficult for us when crossing the Imber ranges.

Any lingering doubts the army authorities may have harboured concerning the desirability of evacuating Imber would certainly have been reinforced in 1942 when one of the worst training disasters of the war took place on the Imber Ranges. The event, a tactical air demonstration before an invited, largely military, audience, was really a full-dress rehearsal before a more prestigious occasion. Within a few days the prime minister, Winston Churchill, was due to arrive with an array of senior officers to witness a similar event.

The demonstration was held on 13 April by the RAF in conjunction with 5 Corps of Southern Command, 'to show the damage that fighter aircraft equipped with cannon and machine guns can do to soldiers on the march, transport columns and tanks.' For this purpose three parallel lines consisting of a number of dummy soldiers, fifteen unserviceable lorries and two tanks were assembled. The spectators formed a fourth parallel 400 yards away from the nearest target. The enclosure, divided into stands, held over 2,000 people and was due to be surrounded by white strips supplied by the army. However, the order for the provision of these strips was not clear. All that could be found on the day was enough material to form a dotted pattern at the front. This fact, plus the involvement of inexperienced and ill-prepared pilots and a confusion of R/T messages, was found by the later Court of Inquiry to be largely responsible for the ensuing disaster.

The objective was to demonstrate the effectiveness of fighter aircraft by attacking the dummy transport column. The exercise commenced at 2 pm with a tactical demonstration without firing. Nine Hurricanes of 175 Squadron, formed just six weeks earlier, then attacked the dummy targets with live ammunition. The first five aircraft completed their run with varying success. The main problem, as one of the pilots later reported, was that it was practically impossible to discern anything while looking into the sun due to the haze. The sixth pilot was 21 year old Sgt William McLachlan, a Canadian, an inexperienced combat pilot who had been posted to 175 Squadron only three weeks before. As he started his dive he was unable to see with clarity the target area, the white ground strips or the spectators' enclosure. He saw what he took to be the dummy troops and lorries and pressed the firing button giving a short burst of about a second. Thinking this was a little short, he raised the hurricane's nose and fired another short burst – directly into the crowd. It was at this point that, seeing the spectators in panic-stricken flight, he realised the full horror of what he had done.

Derrick Mitchell, at school in Warminster, was standing in the playground when this incident occurred. 'I could see right across to Imber Clump', he remembers, 'We could see aircraft ground strafing. When we were going home to Imber later that day it was obvious something had gone horribly wrong. There were at least six ambulances on the Imber road and some on the firing area. By the evening news had got around to the whole village.'

Twenty-five servicemen were killed and seventy-one injured, many seriously, in that tragic accident. Among the injured was Lt the Hon Robert Cecil, the heir of Viscount Cranborne, Secretary of State for the Colonies, who was one of those taken to Warminster Hospital by a fleet of ambulances. Another hospital used for the emergency was Shaftesbury Military Hospital where Henry Crooks, a radiographer, later recalled, 'Of the sixty or so high-ranking officers brought to us many died or were dead on arrival. Doctors, sisters, nurses, VA.D.s and all other ranks worked flat out for several days (and nights) tending to the wounded.'

Undeterred, Winston Churchill insisted on attending a similar display at Imber as planned three days later accompanied by General Marshall, Chief of Staff of the United States Army. This event was accomplished without any further mishap. Sgt McLachlan, the unfortunate pilot found to be directly to blame, was later shot down whilst engaged in a night sortie against enemy shipping near Cherbourg.*

Within the village, people put the horror of this event behind them, continuing to tend the flocks and manage the eternal cycle of agricultural activity from ploughtime to harvest with a workforce depleted by the heavy requirements of war. But at long last something was being done to alleviate the age-old problems of flooding. In 1943, the army commenced a major work programme which Derrick Mitchell remembers clearly:

> It commenced about April. There was a big road widening scheme to make it easier for large military traffic. It caused a great deal of inconvenience. Imber Dock only ran in the winter and was now converted into a large drain as the ditch was in the way. This scheme had not been completed when we left.

In September 1943, the 3rd Armoured Division U.S. Army moved into Warminster and several of the adjoining villages. Much of their training took place on the Warminster and Imber ranges or at West Down. The tide of war was beginning to turn. The greatest multi-national force in history was preparing to invade Europe. With troops from around the globe assembled on the Plain the situation was becoming ever more stressful. A decision was taken to intensify the heavy artillery ranges in the Warminster area which, once again, brought into focus the safety of Imber residents and those living along the Imber corridor. Ladywell and Oxendean Farm to the west, and Cornbury to the east where the Hoopers were living, were among those properties which would be fully exposed to heavy shell fire. The 1,000 yard safety net around the village could no longer be guaranteed; the decision was therefore taken to terminate the tenancy agreements and evacuate the area.

---

*An excellent account of this incident was written by Denis Bateman, a member of the Air Historical Branch of the RAF, in the magazine 'After the Battle' in 1985, a copy of which is available in the Local History Department of Salisbury Library.

When the army called a meeting in the school room on 1 November there was considerable speculation as to the reason. Further announcements concerning the road and drainage scheme was the opinion of the Bell Inn sages. But darker suspicions lay below the surface. 'We knew the Americans were there to do a job – but what? Rumours of invasion had grown so we were aware it was pretty imminent', recalls Derrick Mitchell. 'Householders, farmers, the vicar, and other prominent people were told to attend the meeting. My father was certainly there.' The announcement that the remaining villagers, now numbering around 135, were to be given until 17 December – just 47 days – to leave the village along with all their possessions, came as a complete bombshell, the effect of which can hardly be imagined. The Americans, it was confirmed, needed the village for vital training in street fighting prior to the Invasion.

Derrick recalls the occasion very clearly. 'I remember when they came out of the school room, gathering together in groups to talk about it. Mother was doing washing for Major Whistler at the time and heard from his wife. There was no hostility. Imber people were always docile, hardworking, and took it in their stride once the news had sunk in .'

Haymaking for the last time in 1943. The tractor, with the sweep fixed to the front, belonged to Charlie Hooper of Brown's Farm. The driver, Ellis Daniels, living at Market Lavington, is now 94. The little boy is Alan Ingram.

Reluctantly, but not at this stage embittered, the people of Imber made their preparations to leave. A meeting was held in the Devizes Town Hall on 4 November to explain further why the evacuation was necessary. The army had promised to assist those without alternative accommodation, but most preferred to make their own arrangements with the financial aid allotted to them. Reg Meaden and his family left their quiet cottage and moved to Wincanton leaving the church to the bats. The Wyatts left their smallholding and the small shop that they kept at the west end of the village. 'It nearly broke my heart when we were told to leave', recalled Florence Wyatt later, 'we went to Allington but I never really felt it was my home as Imber was'.

Eva Ketteringham was married at St Giles's in 1921 finding a home at Church View. Her husband was a tractor driver for Sydney Dean before their enforced move to Warminster. Her mother, Emily Goddard, went with them, the oldest inhabitant to be moved. On leaving her home Emily was asked by a local reporter how she felt. 'I lived to die here,' she replied, 'but must is with the King as must was with the Queen when I was young, so I be going to my daughter's at Warminster'. She died two years later and was brought back for burial in the chapel graveyard where her husband Joseph – one of the noted dew pond makers – had previously been laid to rest in 1936.

George Rebbeck was living with his wife and son John in one of the new W. D. cottages when the war started. Called up for service in the navy, he was home on leave when the news of the village evacuation broke. Hearing a knock on the door he opened it to find an army major and a captain standing outside. 'After learning about what was to happen to us I said that I thought it a bit much to come home on leave from fighting for my home only to be told I was losing it!' The army major allegedly replied, 'It's all right, you will probably be back in six months or, at any rate, as soon as the war is over.' Fortunately, the Rebbecks were able to find rooms in Warminster.

And so they prepared their alternative arrangements. The Daniels, Whites, Rebbecks and many other families who had lived and worked in that tiny remote downland village for generations, gathered their belongings ready to begin a new life outside the womblike security of Imber. Enos Matthews had been employed by Sydney Dean all his working life and, like many, had never slept a night away from his cottage. Audrey Streeting

Frances (Frank) Carpenter. Born in Imber in 1886, Frank was a road man for the local council, in the days when great pride was taken in that occupation. He also had a small holding on the outskirts of the village. He was known as 'Tredoodle' because of his lovely singing voice. He was a great churchman although his mother, Priscilla, always went to chapel. He sang in the choir, rang the church bells, dug the graves and always headed the coffin with his bowler hat on! He lived at Cambria Cottage next to the Bell Inn with his wife Edith and daughters Audrey and Marion. Like Harry Meaden, he was a great village character.

(née Carpenter) gives a typical account of the domestic upheavals that were to follow:

> My family lived next to the Bell Inn, on the side going to Warminster, my parents, my sister Marion and me. My father, Francis, was born there – his family went back a long way in Imber. Apart from his smallholding, he worked as a road sweeper – he took great pride over the cleanliness of the village. He was known affectionately as 'Tredoodle', probably because he was always

singing. He had a lovely voice and was in the church choir – as well as ringing the bells, digging graves and heading the coffin at a funeral in his bowler hat. He did a lot for the church. I was born in 1922 and brought up in the village until I was fourteen, when I went as a domestic servant to Sussex for about three years. Then the war started and I joined the A.T.S.

I was at Catterick when the evacuation took place. During that time, which was so awful for my parents, they were unable to find anywhere to go. Eventually, Dad's brother Fred, who was a farrier at Upton Lovell, helped them find a cottage – otherwise they would have been put into communal quarters. Nevertheless, they found it very distressing. Father never really settled and died six years later.

Ron Wyatt was married to my cousin Sylvia Smith with a baby at the time. They were offered accommodation in Edington although it was very poor. Fortunately, Ron was on leave and held out for somewhere better.

One of the saddest to leave was William Walser, rector of the village since 1929 and now 73 years of age. His wife had died at the birth of their only son and he had lived alone in the big stone vicarage for many years. Struggling to get his belongings packed and the valuable church records transferred to a place of safety he had no idea what was to become of him. 'My only son, a cadet, is ill in a military hospital,' he fretted. 'If I were ten years younger I should try for another parish.' Eventually a home was found for him at Bournemouth. David, his son, survived to become Archdeacon of Ely, returning on a number of occasions to take part in the annual services.

Perhaps the most poignant episode concerned the old blacksmith Albie Nash. Albert's family, descended from Imber shepherds, had shoed horses in the village since 1888. During 44 years at the Imber forge he had won many prizes at the county agricultural shows, cherishing in his spare time his beehives and an abundance of flowers to delight passers by. In 1935 he and his wife Martha had left their ancient cottage for one of the new council houses near the Bell, a semi-retirement home with a bath and modern conveniences for the first time. Martha was so proud of it. On the day after the Devizes meeting she could not find him. 'I looked for him in the garden but I found him in the forge. He was slumped over the anvil and crying like a child.' Albie became ill from that day and died a few weeks after the evacuation. The doctor was alleged to have signed his death certificate with a scientific disregard: 'died from a broken heart,' he wrote. Albie was the first resident to return to Imber for burial.

The Nashs' daughter, Gladys, was frantic with worry. Both she and her husband Fred would lose their jobs and the future looked very bleak:

> It was a big upheaval for everyone, but we had to do the best we could. We had to find new jobs and a new home. There was no compensation. We got a few pounds for the vegetables in our garden, but that was all. It was awful. My youngest girl was so upset she refused to go to her new school. People even left belongings in their cupboards because they were so sure they were coming back. I know it sounds silly now to think that we left so willingly, but then we thought we might be helping with the War.

Gradually, the people of Imber departed, to relatives, condemned cottages, almshouses and some to the old workhouses. Others were to find rooms with friends or relatives in the already refugee-packed surrounding villages. Some went to farms. Derrick Mitchell, for example, was lucky. His parents, Fred and Gladys, eventually found a home at Roundway village, Devizes and he worked on Percy Pike's farm there. Ellis Daniels had worked since the age of twelve at Brown's Farm, first for James Hooper and then for his son Charlie. When the grim day of departure came, he was able to move to Charlie Hooper's home farm at Deptford.

The farmers, of course, had the additional worry of disposing of their stock; all sheep, cattle and many farm implements had to be sold. On Saturday, 11 December stock from Seagram's, Brown's and Quebeck Farms were sold off by Woolley and Wallis of Salisbury. 'I remember the day. It snowed, it was foggy, it was awful!' recalls Mollie Archer-Smith. This sale included 842 sheep, carthorses, and 70 head of Sydney Dean's choice dairy cattle – all listed with their pet names. Many implements and much machinery, including harness, barn tackle and dairy utensils, were also disposed of. On the following Wednesday 4,300 breeding ewes and yearlings were sold at Edington, chosen for its close proximity to the railway. 'This sale,' boasted the catalogue, 'presents an exceptionally good opportunity to purchase First Class Cross-bred sheep from some of the healthiest hill farms in Wiltshire' It was not a good opportunity for the Imber farmers. It included all Norris Hooper's breeding flock from Cornbury Farm as 1,100 acres of his grazing

Jack Dean, twin brother to Mollie Archer-Smith, served in the R.A.F. during the Second World War and therefore knew little of the evacuation which took away his family home at Seagram's Farm. He has since developed a successful oil company in Wiltshire.

land was taken over. This forced sale of sheep meant a loss in their value. There were few buyers around as normal sheep fairs, held annually for centuries on a long chain of downland sites from Somerset to Hampshire, took place earlier in the year.

With their stock sold the farmers, too, departed. Major Whistler moved from Imber Court to Everleigh. Capt Arthur Williams, who had commanded the guns on the nearby ranges in World War One and was married to Charlie Hooper's sister Hilda, was forced to move from their home at Browns to a farmhouse at Gores Cross. Sydney and Gladys Dean left Seagrams for Manor Farm at Netheravon, where they continued farming until Sydney's death in 1964. The fields were now silent, the plaintive bleating of sheep permanently muted; descendants of centuries of breeding in some of the best farming country in Britain were heard no more.

In the village, as the 17 December approached, the last rites were taking place. At the chapel, Frank Maidment, the ever-faithful postmaster and Baptist minister from Chitterne, was preparing to take his last service there.

So after 50 years of service to our Lord and His people, through the people having to leave for the troops to have more room to practise, Imber had to finish . . . So on December 5 1943 at 2.30 pm, the last service was held which I conducted, Mr and Mrs Edington taking part, Miss Axford sang a solo, Mr Wyatt gave a short address, and the hymn 'There is a fountain filled with blood' to the tune 'Tucker's Fountain' and a prayer closed the memorial service.

No doubt a similar event was held at St Giles's where another ceremony was to end its long life on a happier note. A marriage took place, that of Bernard Wright, whose family had continued farming at the outlying estate of Ladywell until the end. Phyllis Daniels, his bride, was also from a family long associated with the village, and lived close to the Bell. Bernie worked for Major Whistler at Imber Court Farm. After their marriage they joined the general exodus, making a new home at West Lavington where Bernie worked as a mechanic for Henry Holloway. The marriage took place on the 27 November and the shuttered church closed the following day.

And so, just one week before Christmas 1943, the very last of 'last orders' was called at the Bell Inn. All notices to quit having expired, and all necessary arrangements made, the remaining villagers were forced to leave. They were given a further six weeks in which they could return at specified times to collect possessions but for all intents and purposes the village was dead. A village – given special cohesiveness by its isolation – was dissipated.

Little publicity was given to the event because of wartime restrictions. All doors were shut and barred, the village devoid of human life for the first time since Neolithic times and the land given over 'to rabbits, weeds and modern warfare'. Massingham's little lightship on the Plain had finally been extinguished.

6 A Place of Ghosts

The Villagers had little choice but to leave. After all, nobody could deny that they were living on War Department land now desperately needed for the war effort. There is little doubt that when the inhabitants of Imber departed, so selflessly, from their homes during that bitter 1943-4 winter, it was with a firm conviction that they would be back. Most were buoyed up by the thought that they would return as soon as the U.S. troops had embarked for France.

But after the Invasion came the first forebodings of betrayal. On 29 July 1944, for example, Norris Hooper at Cornbury received a helpful letter from the Command Land Agency at Durrington: 'You will be allowed to harvest any crops on the area which was resumed from you, subject to the conditions which were explained to you in my letter of 7 January 1944 . . .' In July of the following year, however, a letter from the same source was less conciliatory:

> Dear Sir,
>
> In 1944, through the courtesy of the U. S. Forces to whom the use of the Range has been allocated, permission was granted in several instances for the harvesting of crops which had been put in previous to the taking over of Imber Range Area.
>
> This permission of entry was purely temporary and solely for the harvesting of one crop. It did not, and does not, give the right to re-plough or graze any land within the range boundary. The position now is that any person entering on the Imber Range Area without permission is contravening the By-Laws and is committing a civil offence.
>
> The Range Guards and staff have been given instructions strictly to enforce this order and action will be taken in future against any person, other than

military personnel on duty, entering the Imber Range Area unless in possession of a permit signed by the Range Commandant, to whom all applications should be made.

Eventually, after the war's conclusion and the repatriation of the American troops, came the news which was to cause such anger, and sour relations with the local military authorities. The army intended to retain the whole area as a permanent firing range. Re-occupation of the village was impossible as it was required for street-fighting training.

Perhaps there was no legally binding promise from the War Department, although tales of a letter indicating such a declaration continued to abound. Apparently, the story goes, a letter had been posted to all Imber residents before the evacuation only to be retrieved, hastily, by a red-faced military official. Such an exercise, under cover of wartime security, could have been carried out to rectify a potentially embarrassing situation at a later stage.

Nevertheless, there were very firm convictions among Imber folk that *verbal* assurances were given although difficult to confirm over fifty years later and with few of the villagers still alive today. The truth may well be that in getting the residents' cooperation for such an unpleasant change in their circumstances, some of the W.D. personnel involved at the time made statements that were reassuring and over-optimistic – if not deliberately misleading. The villagers, understandably, were only too happy to adjust mentally to those most acceptable to them.

Molly Archer-Smith (née Dean) was 29 at the time of the evacuation. She deplored the fact that there was no written agreement about the villagers' right to return. 'We were given only six weeks to get out,' she recalls wistfully, 'the General gave his word we could come back in six months, but it was only a handshake between gentlemen. When the Army went back on its word, it broke father's heart.' Derrick Mitchell is equally convinced. He was only fifteen when the American troops moved in. 'People had no qualms about leaving because it was for the good of the nation and there was a firm promise that we would soon return. My Mum, Gladys, who worked at Imber Court, was told we would be back before the harvest.' Ellen Carter, postmistress at Imber for 34 years, was told by the two officers in charge of evacuation, 'the whole village is being evacuated for your own safety. You

Mollie Archer-Smith. Until 1943, Mollie had lived all her life at Imber her father, Sydney Dean being one of the principal farmers. However, during the war she served for six years with the First Aid Nursing Yeomanry. 'We didn't do any nursing, only driving!' She was stationed nearby at Urchfont when the evacuation of Imber took place, but later served in Europe after the Invasion. In the picture she is standing in front of the ruins of her old home, Seagram's Farm.

should be away at least three months and you'll be allowed back as soon as possible.'

In June 1947, the *Wiltshire Archaeological and Natural History Magazine* – a most conservative chronicle – observed among its notes:

> To the removal of [Imber's] inhabitants under stress of war we can hardly take exception, but an undertaking was given that they should be reinstated and the fulfilment of that undertaking is still awaited. In the interval the place has been wantonly wrecked. Church, chapel, school, cottages and manor have suffered from the vandalism of persons whose identity is either unknown or unrevealed. Many people became justifiably angry; various Ministries went into a huddle about it, but for a full five months no information has emerged . . .

It was always maintained that, despite the intensity of training prior to the invasion, the Americans treated Imber with as much care as they were able, given the circumstances. It was the British troops most blamed for the damage done in those first years of military occupation. It was also believed that the village was used as a target for bombers and heavy guns, so it is not surprising that the church, chapel, Imber Court and the domestic cottages suffered damage from an early stage.

After the evacuation, the church was boarded up and the graveyard surrounded by barbed wire to give it whatever protection was possible. Nevertheless, misdirected shells made gaps in the walls of cottages and the church was hit by a shell; windows were shattered by the blast despite the shuttering, surplices of the choirboys were blackened and Bibles and hymn books were strewn over the floor. Many of the material possessions at St Giles's were removed at an early stage. The wooden chest, containing the parish registers and churchwardens' accounts book, was stored at Potterne Church. From 1952 the Rous tombs, so admired by Arthur Mee, were housed in Edington church with segments of its ancient glass inserted in a window close by. 'So one corner of another church', it was remarked later, 'is now forever Imber, and Edington marks the 600th anniversary of its own rebuilding by that Act of Piety.' Some of the church woodwork furnished a military chapel at Bratton and the pulpit was placed temporarily in the army chapel at Warminster. This was a prudent measure for in a more quiescent period towards the end of the war unknown hooligans broke into the church and damaged the old tombs and other treasures.

As soon as the war ended, anxious enquiries were made regarding the return of Imber but for a long period no official utterance was made. By this time the sad state of the fabric of the village had become evident. Most damage was due to shell fire and other military activities. Richard Madigan had served in the army throughout the war and had assisted with the evacuation of Imber, finding the task almost as distressing for the troops concerned as for the villagers. 'Everyone had been assured that it was only a temporary measure, and that when the war was over the area would be released and the villagers would eventually be allowed to return.' As the months went by, however, he became less certain :

> After the evacuation our maps were altered and a large red circle was put
> around Imber and instructions were that 'No high explosives are to encroach
> within that circle'. One of my tasks was to ensure that this was carried out. I,

along with others, did our best, but the armies were new, and were training, so mistakes were inevitable.

Many were the times when I would scream aloud to gun crews to 'cease fire' because the shells were landing in a forbidden zone. Many a dirty look did I receive from officers when I, a common unranked soldier, would forbid them to fire again until I had received instructions for them to continue.

Mollie Archer-Smith remembered a large mirror in the drawing room of Imber Court, intact when the Americans departed, but later badly defaced by a scatter of machine gun bullets across it. The bannisters had been torn away from the fine oak staircase. 'Once our parachute regiment had moved in everything was destroyed. Not a bathroom, not a staircase – there was nothing left. They did not mean to give it back to us,' she reflected bitterly.

But there were other factors. The weather had also played its inexorable role. Once the roofs were open to the rain, collapse of the fabric followed very quickly. A certain degree of civilian vandalism – apart from that to the church – was also inevitable in times when building materials were desperately needed; there were plenty ready to provide them by illicit means . Although officially out-of-bounds, it was not difficult for determined intruders to use the old trackways when military exercises were not in progress. W V Dunscombe was the warden of the ranges at that time. When still in the Royal Artillery he had reconnoitred the area before the villagers moved out and was one of those, like Richard Madigan, supervising the evacuation. He had his own convictions regarding the vandalism. 'Of course, you can't blame the W. D. for all the damage,' he observed, 'you know how short building materials were after the war. We used to get chaps driving up with lorries and taking away baths and fittings out of the cottages and stripping lead from the roofs. I reckon civilian spivs did as much damage as any of those street fighting operations.'

In the early autumn of 1947, Monica Hutchings renewed her acquaintanceship with the village, apparently unaware of the ban on civilian entry. Driving along the familiar Warminster road and finding its barrier raised, she pressed on encountering shellholes, deep ruts, and ridges made by armoured vehicles. She was more disturbed by the uncanny stillness; no sheep and no vestige of life, nothing but tank-scarred downs and a white dusty road that grew worse and worse:

At the approach to the village, the outpost trees were gaunt and bare, stripped of all their foliage as by a tornado. They were bleached skeletons of trees . . . The first farmhouse was empty, its roof-tiles missing, the next windowless, with rabbits fleeing through its drunken doorway. For rabbits had taken over possession of Imber. There were droves of them, sweeping across the roadways and gardens, like game on the plains of Kenya. I have never seen so many nor of such a size. Their sway was undisputed, there were scores of them . . . The old houses appeared wounded and hurt, the thatch on my well-remembered wall broken and ruined, the trim gardens overgrown, and the barns and outhouses gaping open to the sky . . .

One solid, well built farmhouse along the road, presumably Seagram's, particularly caught her eye. The creeper which had previously adorned the walls so attractively before the war had now met across both doors and windows presenting a continuous curtain of green.

Miss Hutchings' illegal intrusion was the prologue of much public indignation. Imber became, for the first time, headline news. Lord Long of Wraxall raised the question of the displaced residents of Imber in Parliament. Among the media responses was a picture of one old lady crying into her apron and declaring, 'For we of Imber, broken promises and broken hearts!' Another elderly lady threatened to camp out in the village with a bed and kettle hoping the ravens would feed her as they did Elijah! Arthur Street, the well known broadcaster, author and farmer from Wilton, showed little empathy with the villagers. He was driven there with an army escort but was not much impressed. 'Leave it to the rabbits!' he exclaimed. One journalist drove in his own car which, unlike Monica Hutchings' eleven year old 10 horsepower Wolseley, failed to stand up to the rigours of the rutted and battle-scarred roads and spluttered to a halt.

By this time the army had had enough and refused further access to the press and would be sight-seers. The irrepressible Miss Hutchings, however, was not to be daunted. With one last show of defiance, she by-passed the barriers and went in again covertly with a film director and camera man. Ignoring the 'Beware of Mines' signs and a civil patrol sent to clear the rabbits, they filmed the bleak remains of the village. The civilian contractor proved particularly co-operative, even accompanying her to St Giles's where they tested the bell rope, sending one last despairing clamour echoing across the

Monica Hutchings was the daughter of a 'gentleman's gentleman' (i.e. a butler). She left school with no qualifications but went on to become a writer of books about Wessex. She was passionate about many causes and became involved in both the Imber and Tyneham action groups.

surrounding downland. She escaped along the steep track to Bratton emerging at the head of the White Horse with no more harm than a thick layer of white dust enveloping her ancient car. Nevertheless, such were the images imprinted on her mind that she vowed never to return again. 'Where are the men and women of my own age,' she groaned, 'with whom I once went to school in Warminster?'

It was not until 1948 that the War Office felt compelled to make a statement which was reported in the *Times* of 5 April. After a brief historical background to the situation the statement continued:

Owing to the increased size and range of modern weapons, the 1000 yard safety zone restricted training to such a degree that it was decided that the village would have to be evacuated so that the full Imber area could be used. Although itself not used for any form of training, the village itself has suffered from neglect, accidental damage and weather, and to reinstate it would be very costly. If the inhabitants had been allowed to go back to Imber village the restricted area would have been useless for modern forms of training and as the Imber area as a whole is absolutely vital for training purposes, the decision not to allow the former inhabitants to go back had to be taken.

There is no question of a pledge having been given to the inhabitants that they would go back, but it was understood that, if the War Department ever decided that the village could be given back, the former inhabitants would have first opportunity of taking up their former houses, etc. As this decision to keep the village uninhabited had to be taken, it was consequently decided that street-fighting could take place, but proper arrangements are being made in consultation with the local ecclesiastical authorities to safeguard the church, etc.

Lord Long, one of Imber's champions, took issue with this, claiming that *a verbal pledge* had been given by army spokesmen in the village. He held the army wholly responsible for the destruction of the village. In 1945, he said, a surveyor had estimated that only three months would be required to re-establish it.

So now, it would seem, a scattered and embittered community must resign itself to a life of exile. Occasionally permission was given for groups to return, to gaze forlornly at the mess which had once been their homes, to attend an occasional service at the church, or to stand by the graves of relatives.

Other civilians were permitted entrance only with special army permission. The noted Wiltshire author, Ralph Whitlock, travelled there from his home at Pitton on Easter Monday 1953 when the ranges were not in use. He was shocked by the scene, finding all the cottages shelled, their windows shattered and their gardens returning to nature:

> The old Baptist chapel was fenced off and labelled 'Consecrated Ground' just as was the church, but someone has made a gap through the fence, and the building has been partially ransacked. I went in and saw the pulpit still in position, though much of the floor had gone. A keyboard of an old organ was thrown across the remains of some pews; scraps of books strewn around included leaves of the New Testament and of paper-backed novels; I picked

Imber Court 3 September 1960. Gladys Sutton (nee Dean) surveys the ruins of her old home with her husband and son. Sydney Dean is the man to the right.

up a hymn leaflet evidently used at a forgotten Sunday school anniversary ten or more years ago.

Like Monica Hutchings, Whitlock was conscious of the silence, of a village waiting for the return of children at play and of women gossipping on the way to the shops. But there would be no such return. It was, he said, 'worse than a place of the dead: it is a place of ghosts.'

In 1955 and 56 the villagers were again allowed to return as a group, an occasion leading to further complaints. The oldest ex-residents to attend were Martha Nash, now 78, whose husband Albert had been the first to be

Return to Imber. When 92 year old Bertha Knight died in 1969, her nieces Kathleen Hilary and Gwen Gentry were granted permission to bring the ashes back to Imber. Here they placed them in the Baptist grave-yard with the bodies of Bertha's parents, Harry and Charlotte Meaden.

buried in St Giles's churchyard following the evacuation, and Annie Wyatt whose family had kept the village stores. Capt Williams, the retired gunner from Brown's Farm, was convinced an Act of Parliament prevented Imber being taken over as it had been, but no evidence could be found to support this assertion. 'I felt more confident of going back to Imber when the war was over than I ever felt of anything in my life!' he complained. Many admitted to their resentment at having to apply in writing to visit the graves of relatives or to bury their dead. Gwen Gentry (née Meaden) remembered returning there in 1969 with the ashes of her 92 year old aunt, Bertha Knight, daughter of the old shoemaker Henry Meaden:

> Aunt Bertha had been living at Warminster. She was cremated at Salisbury and I was determined to take her ashes back to Imber. I contacted the War

Office who gave permission to take them on a certain day when there was no firing. My sister Kathleen and a cousin – a Daniels who lived at Westbury – joined me.

Escorted by two tanks, we travelled to Imber. The warden met us and then left us to explore alone as we wished. We found the graveyard, and my grandparent's graves, side by side. We put Aunt Bertha's ashes to join them, said a little prayer and put some flowers above them.

Sometimes the army refused such requests. Mr W J Found from Bristol was a celebrated village cricketer now aged 83. He was born in his grandmother's cottage opposite Imber Court, a home where she, too, had lived until her death 80 years later. He related how in 1954 he had been refused permission to visit the village but had gone there anyway. 'All was quiet so we took the risk and went through from Tilshead. We hardly dared to stop to look. It was a horrible sight and heart-rending to see the destruction and devastation.'

During the group visits in 1955 and 56, the peerless fencing was breached and the church of St Giles opened once more. It was an emotional experience as the *Wiltshire News* observed. 'In the churchyard grey heads of men and women bent over untidy graves, wrinkled hands deftly arranged flowers and tore away weeds and grass. One could sense their full hearts'. Two services were held: at midday and three o'clock on each occasion, a pattern that was to set the tradition for future years. They were described as sincere and straightforward with music provided by an orchestra of local people. (In earlier days Imber had its own string band, possibly the successor to Danny Matthew's 'tin can band'). The services were taken by the Revd Ralph Dudley, vicar of the new combined parish of Edington and Imber, who reassured the congregation that treasures removed from St Giles's were safe at Edington. The two collections, totalling £15, would, he said, pay for the altar to be transported there also. As soldiers stacked away the chairs provided for the occasion, someone remarked that this year there were a few birds in Imber. A hopeful sign. In the previous year there had been none.

By 1960 the services on the Saturday nearest to St Giles's Day had become an annual pilgrimage. The villagers, their faces often tear-stained and grey with grief, were easily distinguished from friends and relations, military observers and the merely curious. This time, however, the congregation had been encouraged by news that the village might be revived. In June of that year the Wiltshire Parish Council Association had asked their Executive Committee to examine the possibility of re-establishing Imber once more as a parish. On a beautiful sunny day, 100 ex-residents arrived accompanied by 200 friends and relatives. But such optimism was soon dashed by news that the service that day would probably be the last held in St Giles's church, which the *Times* reported as being in a state of collapse. The Revd Dudley proposed that the church be moved. 'There are now no people in Imber' he proclaimed, 'and this church with its one service a year does not fulfil its original purpose. I am sure that you who have loved this church will realise that it is better to have Imber moved and used rather than to let it turn into an old ruin.' The School of Infantry at Warminster, it seemed, had suggested that the church be moved there. Not surprisingly, this was not well received. Sydney Dean, still far from settled in his new home at Netheravon, reflected the views of many. 'I would rather see it fall down!' Miss de Glanville Glanfield, sister of a previous Imber vicar, had returned each year to tend her parents' grave and was not prepared to be persuaded into changing her convictions. 'This church does not belong to anyone else. It belongs to the village. I am the last of my line and I want to be buried here.'

By the end of 1960 the battle lines, if not formally drawn, had at least been pencilled in. Villagers, still smarting under the refusal of the authorities to allow them to return to Imber, were now further embittered by the threatened removal of their church, a potent symbol of their hopes for re-instatement. Farmers, notably Sydney Dean, were anxious to return to the land their families had tended for centuries. All that was needed was a catalyst to bring things to a head. This was provided by the War Office and was not so much a spark as a slow burning fuse.

Since 1955 the military authorities had been requesting the Ministry of Transport to make a Draft Order closing permanently the public rights of way in the Imber Range Area. A temporary order, restraining their use on grounds of public safety, had been in use since 1951. Despite a War Office undertaking that the roads and tracks could be restored to public use should the ranges at a later date be closed, there was a growing rumble of discontent.

Such a flagrant restriction of civil liberties was quietly bringing together an unlikely assortment of the good citizens of Middle England to fight for the Imber cause. The end of 1960 was an important staging-post in this conflict for the 31 December brought the ending of DORA – the Defence of the Realm Act – imposed at the outbreak of war in 1939.

NO CRICHEL DOWN AT IMBER!

What you can do . . .

1 Wherever you are—send in the form below. You will then be able to take part in the formation and activities of the association to be set up with the following aims :

> (i) To keep open for public use, the rights-of-way previously closed by the Defence Regulations. To strenuously oppose any Order for their closure.

> (ii) To re-establish the farming and agricultural life of Imber.

> (iii) To re-establish Imber as a civil and ecclesiastical Parish of the County of Wiltshire.

2 Please remember that organisation costs money. This printing costs money. Postage costs money. Much has already been spent in faith. Please help to offset this by sending a donation.

3 If you live in the areas of the Amesbury R.D.C., Devizes R.D.C., Warminster U.D.C., Warminster and Westbury R.D.C., or Westbury R.D.C.—Make sure your council sustains UNQUALIFIED objection to the closure of roads and forces a public enquiry by the War Works Commission. See your local councillor and write to the Clerk of your council asking to be called as a witness for the council (the objector), at any public enquiry into the question of the permanent closure of roads or any later question of the use of Imber.

ASSOCIATION FOR THE RESTORATION OF IMBER

Return this form to Cllr. Austin Underwood, B.E.M., 4, Earls Road, Amesbury, Wilts. Telephone : Amesbury 3001.

Name .... Tel. No. ....

Address ....

I support the aims set out above and wish to be kept informed of the formation and activities of the above Association.

Would you be willing to serve on the committee of this organisation ?.................

I enclose a donation of £   s.   d. to help defray the cost of the organisation.

(Cheques, P.O.s, etc., should be made payable to The Association for the Restoration of Imber)

Printed by Goodwin Press Ltd. (T.U.), 135 Fonthill Road, Finsbury Park, N.4.

Imber protest leaflet, 1961.

7 The 1961 Imber Protest Rally

Cometh the hour, cometh the man. In early January 1961, Amesbury Rural District Council agreed to put up the strongest objections to a provisional Ministry of Transport Draft Order being used to close the roads and other rights of way around Imber permanently. This was largely on the initiative of Councillor Underwood. He was unconvinced by the War Office assertion that the routes might be re-opened at some hypothetical future date when the ranges were no longer required. He insisted that a draft order could not be imposed without a full public inquiry and that is what he demanded.

Austin Underwood was born on 6 September 1918 in a house opposite Amesbury Parish Church where he later served as a choirboy. After primary education in Amesbury, he obtained a scholarship to Bishop Wordsworth's Grammar School, Salisbury. Displaying an early interest in radio, he was encouraged by an uncle to construct his own sets, which led eventually to his becoming a radio ham. Another pastime developed from an early age was the construction of kites. His 1934 diary records him building a five-foot model which he flew with a friend at Milston along the Avon Valley. He had a Hawkeye Box Browning Camera and photographs he took of agricultural scenes and aircraft at Boscombe Down – in those days open to public view – still exist. He then combined these two hobbies by rigging a camera between two kites. This was a plate camera and though it successfully took photographs 'mostly of the tops of trees', none appears to have survived.

In 1937 Lord Radnor offered a prize for a treatise on Town Planning in Salisbury. Cecil Beaton, the celebrated photographer and cultural figure of the day, also offered one for the best illustrations. Austin's project, 60 handwritten pages lavishly illustrated with his own photographs, maps and diagrams, won both prizes and further stimulated his interest in local affairs.

After completing his teacher training at King Alfred's College, Winchester, he took up his first post in Croydon the day after war broke out. The school was immediately evacuated to Brighton but returned later when Austin served during the blitz as a stretcher bearer. He registered as a conscientious objector but the day after he was granted exemption from war service, suffered a change of heart and volunteered for the army. Those who later questioned Austin's loyalty to Britain's land defences would have done well to check his wartime career. He served in the Royal Signals rising to the rank of Foreman of Signals, the equivalent of R.S.M., and took part in the invasion of Europe in 1944 'from the first signal sent from flagship HMS Hilary, to the last sent from Luneburg Heath,' receiving the British Empire Medal for his work at General Montgomery's headquarters. Following V.E. Day he received a posting to India, meeting Nehru, the Indian President, on the way and remaining there until the dropping of the atomic bombs in Japan.

Austin returned to civilian life in the early 1950s to teach at his old school, Bishop Wordsworth's. Gradually he became absorbed in local government at every level although not permitted to serve with the Wiltshire County Council until his retirement from teaching. His passion for social justice involved him in numerous campaigns, notably the CND Movement. He was a founder member of the Committee of 100 and worked closely with Bertrand Russell, attending all the Easter Aldermaston Marches. Such a background would not have endeared him to the Establishment.

Austin's love for the remote village of Imber went back to earlier years especially to cycling trips across the Plain. He later recalled the influence it had on him while serving abroad:

> Most of the men were 'away at the war' and the village of Imber became the softest of targets. In the dust of Normandy or the heat of the Burma hills, Imber was the sleepy kind of village we thought we'd like to go back to. Picnicking up on the downs, or just cycling through from Bratton. We didn't know then, of course, of the fateful meeting in the school on the first of November in 1943. Or the days before Christmas of that year when the people of Imber were moved out. With wartime security few did.

The Defence of the Realm Act had sanctioned any proceedings necessary to acquire and protect such land as the army required. With the cessation of DORA on 31 December 1960, they would need new measures to ensure their hold over the Imber Range area. The War Office, therefore, wished to make permanent the draft order issued by the Ministry of Transport in 1951 temporarily authorising the closure of all highways and footpaths throughout the district and including Imber village. Not surprisingly, this initiative engendered a great deal of opposition, many Wiltshire people considering it a draconian measure. A wave of protest was channelled by the Wiltshire County Council and all local government agencies around the Plain. This general feeling of aggrievement was further aggravated by the disclosure that two local hunts, the Royal Artillery Foxhounds and the Wylye Valley Hunt, as well as private shooting parties, were making full use of the area with impunity.

One person who had no intention of being pressured into a meek acceptance of this measure was Austin Underwood. 'I discovered that the War Office (now the Ministry of Defence) and the Ministry of Transport should both have made proposals concerning the village by this date [31 December, 1960],' he later wrote in the *Salisbury Journal*. 'There is only one way to test the case.' He wrote to the War Office recording his objections and expressing his intentions of walking the road through Imber at the first opportunity. In subsequent letters to the press he went further, outlining his determination to lead a symbolic march through the village and inviting all those interested in the re-establishment of Imber and its surrounding rights of way to accompany him. 'We intend to cross via the main road through Imber, having notified the War Department of our intentions. This is to be a test case, and we would welcome all those who feel strongly on this issue to join us on that date.' The procession was to take place on Sunday, 22 January 1961, commencing at 2.30 pm from Gore Cross on the Salisbury to Devizes Road. In a shrewd counter-measure, Southern Command granted permission for the march to take place – although no such permission had been asked for.

The satirical magazine *Punch*, in its January edition, was quick to respond to the situation with a mock-poem, a parody of Oliver Goldsmith's *The Deserted Village*, and bearing the same title:

Sweet Imber, loneliest village of the Plain
Where yeomen fight to win back their domain,
Where smiling Spring its earliest visits paid,
Followed by tank, bazooka, handgrenade;
Dear lovely bowers of innocence and ease.
Trampled by troopers camouflaged as trees;
Ill fares the land, to hastening ills a prey,
Where trenches scar the tilth of yesterday.

But a bold peasantry, their country's pride,
Too long by Whitehall wizards were denied,
While words of learned length and thund'ring sound,
Kept telling them they could not have their ground,
And still they gazed and still the wonder grew
That such big heads should have so small a clue.

The rally was, of course, a huge political gamble on the part of Councillor Underwood. The capricious English weather, the possibility of a small unenthusiastic attendance, open conflict with a military force, even injury or death by live shells, all these circumstances could have proved disastrous to his campaign. In fact the protest rally proved a triumph. It was observed by the broadcaster McDonald Hastings, a member of the huge media presence on that day, that in any other country this challenge by indignant individuals to the establishment of the State would have been the occasion of a confrontation with armed police and possibly violence. Whether the authorities had not envisaged such a show of strength, it is astonishing that there was not a single policeman or uniformed soldier to provide even a token presence. In the event, there was no need. The procession of vehicles, in excess of 700, pouring off the main Devizes Road at Gore Cross, was well managed by the marshals who received good-natured co-operation throughout the day.

There was an air of excitement and expectation as vehicles queued along the track to commence the procession. Two tables had been erected to enable visitors to register their attendance and their objections to the proposal to close the rights of way. The army maintained a low profile, emerging from the shadows only when occasion demanded or to put the

Section of the petition signed by participants in the first Imber Protest rally on 22 January, 1961.

military point of view. As the organisers made ready for the winding journey across the downs to Imber, the Range Officer arrived complete with powerful loudspeaker. He informed the assembly that the road along which they would pass had been especially cleared to ensure their safety. 'Under no circumstances should you leave the road because the ground has not been cleared and is not safe,' he warned. Neither were they to enter the houses in the village which were equally unsafe. Both warnings were met with jeers and gales of laughter and subsequently ignored by a section of the crowd out to get the most from their day.

An army spokesman then addressed members of the press explaining the WO purchase of the land from 1929-32 and its subsequent involvement in the area. No such promise of a return to the village had been given, he said, merely an assurance that if Imber should become available, they would have the first opportunity to do so. For 330 days in the year the ranges were used by the regular and territorial armies. A considerable amount of firing took place and the use of the ranges would increase when the Small Arms Wing of the School of Infantry moved from Hythe to Warminster in the following year. Neither could the army train elsewhere in the country nor abroad as had been suggested. This would prove wildly expensive.

Because of the threatening weather and the needs of television and cameramen to use the remaining light, the expected short meeting outlining the day was cancelled and the protest march commenced. What a spectacle it must have produced! Various estimates recorded vehicles in excess of 350 cars and a similar number of vans crawling bumper to bumper through a landscape invaded by scrubland, across the mud-churned tracks to Imber, stopping momentarily to offer lifts to the hundreds of foot travellers. Motor cycles, scooters and pedal cycles wove between slower vehicles skidding on the greasy surface. A three-mile queue moved turgidly forward past fields criss-crossed with tank and lorry tracks, derelict buildings and triangular notices along the verges warning 'TO LEAVE THE ROAD IS DANGEROUS' and ' THERE ARE MISSILES THAT CAN KILL'. At the army barrier boys of Dauntsey's Public School, resplendent in their uniforms and boaters and out for an adventurous day, were stopped by prefects; only a small group of the seniors were permitted to go farther.

The first Imber Protest Rally, Sunday 22 January, 1961. Henry Wills, the senior photographer of the Salisbury Journal, took this picture of the crowds arriving at the village. The tractor, which led the way, was driven by Richard Hooper, son of Norris and Betty Hooper from Cornbury Farm. Austin Underwood is standing behind him.

Barely a mile from Imber a tractor waited under the leaden sky. It was driven by Richard Hooper, the latest of the long line of his family to farm in the area. When the convoy, now snaking back to Gore Cross, had finally arrived, the tractor roared into life and slowly led the way forward into Imber. It was pulling a plough, a powerful symbol to the demonstrators of their desire to see the land returned to agriculture. Following closely behind was the main party, a phalanx of farmers like Sydney Dean and others from surrounding farms, accompanied by their employees, ex-residents from the village, representatives of local authorities and other interested bodies.

Stumbling through thick mud the column made its way through the crumbling remnants of mud-walled cottages to the very centre of the village. Back along the track, the queue of vehicles still stretched as far as the eye could see, its drivers and passengers having to complete their journey on foot. As the crowd surged through the village, a green flag bearing the slogan 'Forever Imber' was hoisted to the WD warning masts at each end. The crowd cheered good humouredly, further evidence that this was no rag, tag and bobtail element out to create havoc, but a well-organised representation of Middle England, as the *Guardian* was to point out the following day:

> And if the Minister of War about whom they made so many jokes had been there, he would probably have admitted that they looked like a sensible, honest cross-section of the Wiltshire farming community. It was not a march for the professional 'anti's' but for ordinary people with strong feelings, for men and women who felt that a piece of land and a dead village could be put to better use. There were men in tweeds – many of them remembering days when the downs around Imber grew crops more profitable than the present harvest of derelict tanks – staid housewives, students, school boys on bicycles, and representatives of the old Imber farms.

Within the village, Austin Underwood had wasted no time in creating an atmosphere most calculated to inspire the emotional response he desired. He produced a large notice and nailed it prominently to one of the devastated walls. 'NOTICE TO QUIT' it read. 'We the people hereby serve notice on the War Department to vacate and deliver up to the county of Wiltshire the parish of Imber'. A newly-restored Bell Inn sign was hung in its old position. Some drank a toast in orange juice in the battered hostelry recalling earlier memories. For years Ushers, the Trowbridge Brewery had renewed its licence in the hope of better days, but now it was in the possession of the War Department. As people climbed curiously into shell-shattered houses and tramped across long-neglected meadows in defiance of the army warnings,

A group of old Imber residents at the first Imber Protest Rally suitably equipped!

Councillor Underwood propped up a shell fragment on a derelict wall. 'A monument to War Office stupidity!' he proclaimed.

Returning residents to Imber must have experienced very mixed emotions on that day, seeing the destruction and decay to their old homes, some probably for the first time. Seventy-eight year old William Burgess had worked for Sydney Dean at Seagram's Farm. Married at St Giles's Church, he had lived his life peacefully in the village throughout his previous life and been one of the last to leave. 'I would like to come back here to live', he reflected, 'but I don't see much hope.' This sentiment was also expressed by Ellen Carter, also 78, from West Lavington. Postmistress for 34 years, she had returned with her friend Nellie Coleman of Warminster whose parents and grandparents had lived their lives there too. Mrs Joan Sanderson (née Ferris) kept a general store at Wylye but exclaimed, 'I spent four of the happiest years of my life here from 1931-5. I should love to come back and open a shop.' Mr M P Knubley, a 76 year old retired District Valuer from North Bradley, recalled the days when his cousin, Mr A G Hartley, rented Parsonage Farmhouse and held shooting parties over the fields, followed by high tea with Devizes cheese cakes as the main delicacy. Wistfully recounting their memories to all who cared to listen, the ageing residents of Imber tramped over the shell-torn landscape to Church Lane and the decaying fabric of St Giles's – ironically, it was recalled, the patron saint of cripples.

An estimated 2,000 people, or more, had attended the day, around 200 of them with strong Imber connections. Although most of the demonstrators came from within Wiltshire, others had travelled considerable distances to be there. Many were from the London area, others from as far away as Liverpool and the Midlands. Mr and Mrs A Weller, for example, drove 120 miles from Lewes in Sussex. Mrs Weller had lived at Imber until she met her husband whilst he was serving nearby in the 1914-18 war. 'When my parents were moved 18 years ago they were told, and so were all the others, that they would be able to come back', she remarked bitterly. 'It never happened and they are dead now'. Her husband, a farmer, said, 'It was a lovely village when I knew it and the land is some of the finest I know. I have never seen such corn as used to grow here. It was as tall as me!'

Austin Underwood had delved deeply into his past experiences in order to plan this rally; experience with the army, with education and with local government. All had helped him prepare for this day which was the outcome of nearly a month's work and a great deal of money which he had so far borne himself. Now, standing in the crumbling ruins of a battle-torn cottage, he joked with the exploring protesters, refuting the military claims

A section of the crowd at Imber on the 22 January, 1961. Austin Underwood's Morris Traveller can be seen in the foreground and he is addressing the crowd from a position just behind it.

to the church, the village and the rights of way. If the army had driven an armoured vehicle in front of the plough, as had been rumoured, it would never have moved, he asserted, because people would have been sitting all around it!

Then, as crowds stood expectantly in the roadway and on the banks around the ruins of the old post office, Mr Underwood commenced his half hour speech. 'This is a wonderful gathering but it is only the beginning,' he exclaimed. 'We aim to force an Inquiry and we say to the War Department "For God's sake go and let the farmers and farm workers cultivate the land again." Do they think this is some Polish village they can grind under their heel?'

Aware of the low-key presence of military officers in civilian garb, he continued by emphasising that this was no protest because they were there as a legitmate right since the Defence Regulations had ended. 'Isn't it wonderful! Here are the army vehicles, the people in control at the War Office and they are powerless. Here are we, together with them, back in Imber. Visit the church and the remains of what was Imber. Reclaim your heritage!'. It was the rhetoric of confrontation and the crowd responded accordingly.

Using a microphone to address the meeting, Councillor Underwood referred to the apologies, almost 100, which he had received from non-attenders. Most prominent among these had been Lord Long of Wraxall, who had fought long and hard for the return of the village in the House of Lords. He wished them better luck then he had had in his three-year fight to regain the land. The poet John Betjeman had also written referring to vast areas of remote England laid waste, some still held by the military authorities which was a scandal! He urged them to fight on. 'Wiltshire and the rolling downs for ever!' he concluded.

Referring to the famous incident in 1839 when Matthew Dean, the Imber farmer, had been attacked by thieves, Mr Underwood claimed, 'It was a century after that incident that the descendants of Mr Dean were robbed of their land by the War Department . . . We want an inquiry and we aim to force an inquiry. Let the War Department put their case and show how the horses and hounds can be immune from the danger of the area when the public are told they must not roam about because of the dangers . . .' It was sheer chicanery, he said, for the War Department to say that the draft

The first Imber Protest Rally. Austin Underwood addressing the crowds in the village.

order by the Ministry of Transport enabled them to continue to stop people from using the roads, as such a stand could not be enforced until an inquiry had been held. 'Where is the War Department now?' he asked 'The War Department is a laughing stock because not one of you has got a pass!'

Spurred on by a cheering crowd growing larger as more and more latecomers arrived, he continued to rail at the military authorities. His comparison of them with the Boy Scout movement did him no good (a general apology was later released by him to the press) but his words certainly struck a note with the gathering. Accusing the War Department of neglecting the church and wanting to remove it, he gave an impassioned response. 'If the stones cannot cry out, then the men must cry out. I will be one and there will be hundreds and thousands more. You have seen Imber today perhaps for the first time and it is not as the War Department try to represent, a desolate area with mines where you dare not go off the road.'

With the crowd now thoroughly roused, other speakers were brought to the microphone. Monica Hutchings, the author, forgoing her promise never to return to Imber again, spoke of her earlier visits and her admiration for its fertile soil. 'Let the army use land on which nothing will grow,' she exclaimed, 'the Services own one seventh of the whole acreage of this one

County. I think it is too much.' She added, 'Some of you have come here for the sensation. Some of you have come for a jolly day out, but I believe the vast majority sincerely want the army out of here.'

Richard Clitheroe, a councillor from Liverpool and the national organiser of the League Against Cruel Sports, had long campaigned for the return of land to agriculture. He understood that the WO had its spies there that day and challenged them to serve a writ on him for trespass – under the regulations that no longer existed! We had, he said, given our church and park railings and our land in the cause of freedom during the war. We nearly gave our heritage in the fight for freedom and it was with that freedom that they were now urging the return of Imber.

Daniel Sargent, now 87, and living in Salisbury, had previously been a member of the Devizes Rural District Council and Salisbury Rural District Council. He said his family had farmed 25,000 acres around Imber, a considerable area. 'We are patriotic citizens,' he said in a firm voice, 'and we don't wish to be trodden on.' From the Isle of Wight came Mr Lewis who, as a billeting officer during the war, had been responsible to Warminster and Westbury Rural District Council for the evacuation of the village. 'I hope it will not be long before all the farmers, their workers and their families return here and carry on their work,' he said. Mr J H Marti, a member of Melksham UDC, outlined the struggle his authority had encountered with Wiltshire County Council over the closure of footpaths but had won after an inquiry from Whitehall. He was confident the present fight could also be won.

Amid the general excitement of the crowd, it was a former Imber resident who next came to the microphone, a Wiltshire farmer who, in a steady voice which belied his 77 years, tried to remind his audience what this was fundamentally about. Sydney Dean's family had farmed at Imber for over two centuries. During that time they had performed civic and religious duties in a constant succession as well as tending sheep and cattle and producing corn of the finest quality. 'I had six weeks to get everything out,' he remembered. Although ready and willing to start re-cultivating the land he lost in 1943, reason told him otherwise. 'I know I shall not be able to get here again,' he said, 'but I should like to know that my sons and daughters can return to Imber.' Fred Daniels, a past worker at Seagram's now living near Warminster, readily supported him.

At the conclusion of the speeches, Mr Underwood asked for a vote – yes or no – for the establishment of a support group: an Association for the Restoration of Imber. Hundreds of voices roared 'Aye'. There seemed to be no dissenters and the proposal was carried unanimously. Its aims were quite clear:

*To keep open all rights of way in the Imber area and strenuously oppose any move to close them

*To re-establish the farms and agricultural life of Imber

*To re-establish Imber as a civil and ecclesiastical parish

A collection of £38 was then taken to further the campaign.

As the rally drew to its conclusion, a gramophone recording of the old church bells rang out in triumph over a village deprived of them for eighteen years. A short service conducted by the Edington vicar, Revd Ralph Dudley, included the hymn, 'The Church's One Foundation', and prayers for blessings upon the land and those who determined its use. A minute's silence was then observed, 'to the memory of centuries of craftsmanship and husbandry the military had destroyed; to those who were evicted in 1943; and to those who had died heartbroken before they could return to Imber.'

In the deepening dusk a convoy set off along the pitted Warminster road for a final motorcade and meeting which would provide an opportunity to see Monica Hutchings' earlier film on the village. 'We expected 200 people and we got 1,000 more!' cried the triumphant Mr Underwood as he drove up and down the line of cars, urging drivers to stay in convoy through Warminster, 'to show the people how we feel.'

Others returned the way they had come, along the tracks to Bratton, Heytesbury or Gore Cross. Many hardened and enthusiastic walkers had trekked into the village along numerous other rights of way, people determined to express their free passage along the footpaths for the first time since the prohibition had been imposed, and were now returning the same way. A party of ramblers, for example, formed themselves into a group to walk from Erlestoke, a distance of three and a half miles each way.

Most, however, returned to Gore Cross, back over the downland, past the ruins of discarded tanks and military vehicles, and the warning notices, through the vedette check post with its white barrier raised in the air. As they turned for one last look at the route they had taken from the now silent and deserted village, they saw through the gathering dusk the ominous warning sign, 'RANGES NEXT IN USE 0800 HOURS MONDAY JANUARY 23'.

Austin placing his notice to the War Office on the side of the Bell Inn.

8 Forever Imber

The military presence at the January Rally had been consciously low key. The response afterwards was similarly muted. A Southern Command spokesman, who had watched the events unfold, remarked to the press: 'We are concerned over the real danger that exists on the ranges that are in use for 330 days of the year . . . Any incitement to trespass further will be rather unfortunate because we are not exaggerating the danger that exists here'.

But Councillor Underwood was not to be diverted from the wave of enthusiasm that his initiative had unleashed. 'I have not asked people to wander over the ranges – which horses and hounds and shoots seem to use safely', he retorted. 'I have stated that a large body of people are determined to use the roads from now on. It is the duty of the War Office to see that the roads are not obstructed or made dangerous'. The League Against Cruel Sports was also quick to take up this point outlining their objections in a letter to John Profumo, Minister for War. Many others went into print supporting the call for a public inquiry into the proposed closure of the roads. 'The onus of proof of the need to close the roads should be on the War Office, right of access by the public being assumed', wrote Terry Heffernan of Durrington. 'At present, however, right of closure by the W.O. is being assumed and there appears to be little chance of the public having the opportunity to prove right of access'. Another correspondent described Imber as a symbol of the society in which we live. 'Is it not a mockery that in a society which we call "free", a government department can evict a whole community of people in order to sterilise a tract of land?'

On Saturday, 11 February, the inaugural meeting of the Association for the Restoration of Imber was held at Devizes Town Hall. Its aims remained

IMBER
SHALL LIVE !

1941

● KEEP OPEN THE ROADS

On the ending of the Defence Regulations, the War Department have applied for an Order to **PERMANENTLY** stop up all rights of way through the Imber area. A huge area is in danger of being erased from the map of Wiltshire for ever. No rider can be added to the Order if granted. " Assurances " that roads could be re-opened at some future date would be legally worthless. The Order can only be either granted or refused. It must be refused or these roads and all other rights of way will be lost for ever.

The Minister of Transport has promised that a public inquiry will be held into the application.

● SAVE THE CHURCH OF ST. GILES

Eighteen years of occupation of Imber has meant neglect of the church. We urge that the War Department should put it in good order for future generations.

● PRESERVE OUR HERITAGE

A promise was made that the people of Imber should have the opportunity to return. Farmers are ready to begin farming the sterile acres today. We must ensure that the promise is honoured. This is one of the richest archaeological areas in Britian ; one of the richest farming areas of Wiltshire. It must eventually be returned.

1961

WHAT YOU CAN DO :

1. Write to the Minister of Transport **N O W** and object to the making of the order to stop up the rights of way.

2. Enlist the support of your M.P. **N O W**.

3. Ensure that your local council will sustain their objection at the inquiry. If you live in the Amesbury R.D., Devizes R.D., Warminster U.D., Warminster and Westbury R.D. or Westbury U.D., write to the Clerk and tackle your local member **N O W**.

4. Help the Association for the Restoration of Imber with your financial support.

Return to the Hon. Secretary, Association for the Restoration of Imber,
4 Earls Road, Amesbury, Wilts.   Tel. Amesbury 3001.

Please keep me informed of the activities of the Association :

Name

Address

I enclose a donation of £   :   s.   d. towards the Association's funds.
(Cheques, P.Os., etc. should be made payable to the Association for the Restoration of Imber and addressed to the Hon. Treasurer at Homerfield, Beauclerc Street, Devizes, Wilts).

S.P. 29002

Above and opposite: Publicity material advertising the Forever Imber campaign and rallies,
1961

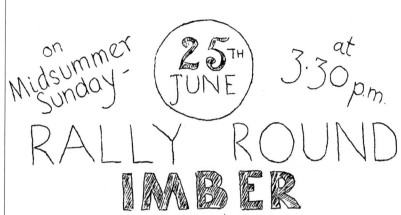

on Midsummer Sunday -
25ᵀᴴ JUNE
at 3·30 p.m.

RALLY ROUND
IMBER
-come to
WHITE HORSE HILL, BRATTON, Westbury, Wilts.

with BRATTON SILVER BAND

MOTORISTS! assemble GORE CROSS 2·0-2·30 p.m.
for the CAR CONVOY ROUTE: Main road, via.
Tilshead, Chitterne,
Heytesbury, Warminster, Westbury, White Horse Hill.

THE WILTSHIRE COUNTY COUNCIL HAVE BETRAYED the rights of way -
By a vote of 31-38 - 7 meagre votes - they have withdrawn their objection
to the closing of the roads at the public inquiry.

THE CHAIRMAN REFUSED A RECORDED VOTE - Were the 38 ashamed of their vote ?

A COUNTY COUNCILLOR SAID AFTERWARDS: "I agree that we shouldn't give up
the roads, but I couldn't vote against the W.D. " !

ROLL OF HONOUR

THESE HAVE NOT JOINED THE BETRAYAL : Amesbury R.D.C., Some local Parish
Councils, The Wiltshire Branch Parish Councils' Association, The
Association for the Restoration of Imber and some individual objectors.

FORWARD TO THE PUBLIC INQUIRY ! WE FIGHT ON ! JOIN US ON JUNE 25th.

The Association for the Restoration of Imber, 4, Earls Road, Amesbury,
Wilts. Telephone: Amesbury 3001.

as outlined at the January rally: to re-open the 57 rights of way across the ranges, to re-establish farming and to restore the village as a civil and ecclesiastical parish. Efforts would also be made to ensure the church of St Giles was kept in good repair. Having been elected general secretary, Austin Underwood now had, in addition to the support of Amesbury Rural District Council, a further platform from which he could continue a purposeful campaign. The committee of eleven included George Phillips as assistant secretary, Frank Weaver, a retired bank official from Devizes as treasurer and Fred Parker, the chairman of Bratton Parish Council, subsequently elected as chairman. Among the vice-presidents were the authors John Betjeman, Ralph Whitlock and Monica Hutchings. Another, Philip Noel-Baker, was the M P for Swindon. Brian Tilley, the Mayor of Devizes, presided at the meeting and wished the association well in its efforts to initiate a public inquiry. 'Quite often,' he said, 'groups which have very small beginnings like this - although they might be an embarrassment to certain people in official organisations – are the pulsation of our democratic system.'

Councillor Underwood immediately gave notice that the ARI would continue to fight the Draft Order to close the Imber roads. To this end the three most local M Ps, Sir Robert Grimston representing Westbury, Percival Potts of Devizes and John Morrison for Salisbury, were to be approached, hopefully, for their support. With grim determination, the Committee commenced to plan a plethora of activities to ensure a high profile for their campaign. Building on the success of the rally, a series of monthly drives through Imber was to be arranged with other open air events as the warmer weather arrived. Promotional pamphlets labelled 'FOREVER IMBER' show these to have included a May gathering on White Horse Hill with Bratton Silver Band in attendance, and a national car rally through the village. At Imber itself a Midsummer Fair was contemplated with a cricket match between an All-England XI (to be captained by Dennis Compton) and a team to include old Imberians. As Druids celebrated the Solstice, a dawn convoy would leave Stonehenge at 5 am en route for Imber led by James Duncan of Romsey, said to be the oldest Druid in the world, resplendent in his robes.

Once more unsolicited approval from the WO was forthcoming for the second rally on 26 February, an event severely dampened by torrential rain which kept walkers and cyclists to a minimum. The number of cars and vans which turned out, however, were almost as many as the previous event. There was to be no meeting at Imber this time and trenches cut by the army along the Warminster road restricted the traffic to one way only commencing at Gore Cross. With rain lashing across the open windtorn downland, the convoy found much of the roadside churned into mud. At the end of the route about 60 vehicles remained to follow Austin Underwood's loudspeaker van through the sodden streets of Warminster though less than 30 stuck it out until the end. The press, as bedraggled as the rest, observed wryly that if 22 January was to be known as Imber Day, then this should be remembered as Umbrella Sunday, a minor festival in the civil liberties calendar!

On 1 March the question of the re-instatement of Imber was raised in Parliament by Philip Noel-Baker who enquired of the Secretary of State for War when he intended to restore Imber to the civilian population in view of public feeling. John Profumo replied emphatically that it was impossible as the area was needed for training the Strategic Reserve, the School of Infantry and other units. 'The whole of the present Imber training area, in the middle of which the village lies, is essential for this purpose and there is no alternative to it.'

Undaunted by this, the ARI put in hand its plan for the third drive on 26 March. This time all four roads into Imber would be used. In addition, parties of ramblers would walk the footpaths, groups of horse riders would use the bridleways and vehicles using other tracks would ensure that all 57 routes were covered. Austin, himself a licensed radio operator, was to organise a mobile radio network to synchronise the whole operation. Defiantly he proclaimed that this was their answer to Mr Profumo's unfeeling statement in the House of Commons and would prove a greater blow to the morale of the W O than the rally in January.

But the War Office had had enough. On 15 March John Profumo, soon to be disgraced for misleading Parliament over the Christine Keeler affair, sent a confidential memorandum to the Prime Minister, Harold Macmillan. It made quite clear his personal view of Councillor Underwood:

> We are running into some trouble about the Imber training area and I think you would wish to know the position as there is bound to be some more publicity.

> There has been a move to get us to give up the training area. The organiser is one Councillor Underwood. He is a bad man, very Left Wing and an Aldermaston marcher, but he has managed to rally a good deal of support. He and his cronies have already held two or three demonstrations in and around the village of Imber with our permission at times when the ranges were not being used.
>
> The trouble now arises because he wants to hold a mass rally on Sunday 26 March. We have had to refuse permission because an annual Territorial Army course, involving live firing all day, takes place that Sunday. It has been arranged for many months and it would be extremely inconvenient to alter it now.
>
> Underwood has been told, but insists that he proposes to hold the rally come what may.
>
> I have decided we must apply for an injunction to restrain him and his colleagues. I have taken advice of the Treasury Counsel and I have asked that the Attorney-General should be consulted. I expect we shall get an interim injunction on Friday and thereafter some publicity may arise. . .

This laid down the framework for subsequent action. Southern Command HQ at Wilton informed Austin that such a course on 26 March was out of the question. On that date live firing would be taking place, the final phase of a course for T.A. units and cadet officers organised some months previously. This would mean the firing of shell and small arms ammunition in considerable quantities throughout the day in an area which had Imber as its centre. The proposed veteran car rally on 14 May was also unacceptable as the range was scheduled for an all-day Civil Defence exercise.

Councillor Underwood declared his intention of continuing the events anyway. On 26 March a special group of volunteers from the ARI would be assigned to force their way to the village whatever the circumstances. The volunteer party would travel by Land Rover and on foot in order to hoist the green 'FOREVER IMBER' flag on a WD mast in the village. In addition, the pre-arranged groups would travel there on foot, horseback and car using every available track as well as the roads from Gore Cross, Bratton, Warminster, Heytesbury, Erlestoke, West Lavington and Tilshead Lodge.

This attempt by Austin Underwood to brazen it out was the point at which the authorities decided that matters had gone far enough. The civil disobedience displayed by a group of local farmers and other disenchanted citizens, no matter how respected, could no longer be regarded as the rustic gestures of a comic opera. (A comparison made even more risible by the West Wilts Bacon Producers' Association's decision to make the church of St Giles its emblem with the rallying slogan IMBER BRAND!) A whiff of gunpowder had been fired across the bows of the War Office. The security of its training programme was being threatened and a more direct response would have to be made.

On Friday 24 March the War Office applied to the High Court for an injunction restraining the officials of the ARI, or others, from entering the Imber Range area. An interim injunction, refusing entry to the rights of way through Imber, was granted until a full hearing could be arranged and the ARI had no lawful alternative but to abide by it. A television debate between Austin and a representative of the War Office was also called off when the official, under orders, withdrew. The ARI responded with a nationwide appeal to fight the High Court action. A deputation of its officials and three of the oldest former residents of Imber met with their local M Ps at the House of Commons. The response was predictable but not unreasonable: the honourable members would not interfere with the needs of the defence training but would support an early public inquiry to clarify the position of the rights of way and request that the church be properly maintained.

In response to the injunction, the third rally was cancelled. At every venue where the ARI had notified the War Department that they would assemble, the Association placed notices saying 'Emergency Plan Cancelled'. In addition, their marshals were at hand to turn back any cars or walkers who had not received the news. Despite this action, the army was out in force with a radio control at every point and with a helicopter hovering overhead. Not content with this, a covert operation seems to have been adopted by the WO at this stage.

The main officials of the association complained of being 'shadowed' by mysterious plain clothed men. Frank Weaver, the association's treasurer, was particularly incensed by this behaviour. When he and his wife awoke on the day of the cancelled rally, they were surprised to find three strange cars, with male occupants, parked at different positions along Beauclerc Street, Devizes, where they lived. Mrs Weaver told the *Wiltshire Gazette and Herald*

An army checkpoint at Gore Cross after the cancellation of the March Rally. At each
assembly point both army and ARI marshalls were on duty to turn people back. Austin
Underwood's Morris Traveller can be seen to the right and an army Saracen Armoured
Personnel Carrier to the left.

reporter how they were subsequently followed to church by these vehicles.
'They waited outside during the service and positioned their cars so that each
entrance to the churchyard was under watch. When we left the church they
escorted us back to our homes.' Her husband, who was the church organist,
later went to a practice of the Devizes Musical and Philharmonic Society of
which he was conductor, and one of the cars remained in attendance outside.
None of the men disclosed their identity. George Phillips, the association's
assistant secretary, was also watched by two men, one with a false press
card. They, too, refused to reveal their identities.

Things came to a head at an open-air meeting arranged in place of
the prohibited drive-through. This had been organised by the ARI to take
place on the Green at Devizes where plain-clothed observers made notes and
took photographs of the proceedings. Mrs Ormond, a committee member,
later described them to members of the Wiltshire Parish Council Association
as, 'the most extraordinary people, men in plain clothes and enormous boots
who went around looking very fearsome at people. We were all treated

as though we had sub-machine guns under our coats.' The Association's chairman, Fred Parker, protested at this behaviour, emphasising that they were doing nothing to interfere with the High Court action. The main point of the meeting had been to announce an appeal for funds.

The executive committee of the League Against Cruel Sports, continuing its objections to hunting on the ranges, were also targeted. They later protested to Mr Profumo at the treatment received by the League's chairman and five other members using the public highway outside the perimeter of the battle area. Among incidents reported were the activities of a spotter plane and 'spy teams' with walkie-talkies relaying details of their vehicles to an unknown source. Security police even followed their members into a public toilet in order to overhear their conversations!

Mrs Sophie Annetts (née Volkov), who exercised her dogs on the range before the injunction, was also an ARI member She remembers the period as a particularly unhappy one:

> I always loved Imber, snuggled into a fold of such beautiful hills, but this was a scary campaign. As far as I was concerned the fight was for the footpaths and the legal right to walk the country as we chose. We felt the full weight of the special services observing our every movement as if we were a threat to national security. I am sure our 'phones were tapped. Our cars were followed. Probably we were on a list of undesirables.'

In early June, the Wiltshire County Council decided by a slender majority to withdraw its previous objection to the closing of the Imber Range rights of way after an understanding with the War Department that the roads would be returned to the County 'if and when' the W D no longer required them. This decision was subsequently endorsed by Devizes Rural District Council and was a bitter blow to the ARI and the Wiltshire Association of Parish Councils which had maintained their objections to the closure. Councillor Underwood described the move as a betrayal of the trust placed on them as guardians of the rights of way, a point he put again at the Midsummer rally held on Sunday, 25 June on White Horse Hill.

'RALLY AROUND IMBER' began once more as a car convoy which assembled at Gore Cross, this time travelling a 25 mile route along main roads through Tilshead, Chitterne, Westbury and Bratton to avoid the forbidden route. Two accidents marred the journey, one involving a collision with a bubble car whose driver was taken to hospital with head injuries. In heatwave conditions, 300 people assembled on an area above the Westbury White Horse on Bratton Down, a symbol of ancient Saxon resistance. Situated about 100 yards from the Imber Range boundary – just about as close as the Association dared go – the crowd enjoyed a picnic in the sunshine and listened to medleys from the Bratton Silver Band as they waited to hear Francis Noel-Baker. In his speech the MP for Swindon offered to lead a deputation to meet the Secretary of State for War. He also criticised the other local MPs who, he said, had made no attempt to carry the banner for Imber in the Commons. This later produced a sharp rejoinder from Sir Robert Grimston's agent who said Sir Robert had dealt with various ministries and asked questions in the House. Several other speakers, including Stanley Dyer, a County Councillor, and the author Monica Hutchings addressed the crowd which gathered under the familiar green ARI flag flying from a 30-foot steel mast.

Austin Underwood would have sensed at this stage that enthusiasm was waning. 'RALLY AROUND IMBER' had not attracted the media attention which he had hoped for, the decision of Wiltshire County Council and Devizes RDC to reach a compromise position with the War Office, the apparent reluctance of other local authorities to commit funds for legal representation at the coming High Court hearing – all these factors would have had a disheartening effect. The ARI was now pursuing its hopes of further support from among candidates in local elections and upon a mobile exhibition which had begun its tour at the West Wilts Agricultural Show at Melksham.

Sufficient funds were raised to brief counsel for the High Court hearing but to little avail. The Draft Order was confirmed and judge, Mr Justice Paull, awarded costs against the ARI after granting a declaration to the War Office that members of the ARI were not entitled to enter or pass through Imber Firing Ranges without the Crown's consent, an undertaking the Association had to accept. Their counsel, Mr J A S Toogood, gave the necessary assurances on their behalf and spoke of the great courtesy and consideration shown to the defendants by the W O at all times. It might have been a handshake at the end of a typically-English game of rugger.

Francis Noel-Baker, M.P. for Swindon, addressing the crowd on White Horse Hill at the Midsummer 'Rally Around Imber' event on Sunday 25 June 1961.

All Austin's hopes were now pinned on a public inquiry. As he pointed out, the W O had not been given permission to close the highways permanently. The Warminster to Gore Cross road, moreover, had been an important link road for people travelling to and from the west. Further efforts were made to raise the necessary funds for a barrister to present their case. Amesbury Rural District Council had supported the campaign throughout, aware that a number of displaced Imber residents were living within their area, but others were more reluctant to part with their money. Austin suggested that other local authorities combine with Amesbury to present their case, a procedure which would cut costs but still allow for an individual response.

When the Revd Ralph Dudley took the September services at St Giles's that year it was in a church sadly in need of repair. Brilliant sun streaming through plain glass windows, cracked and shattered, revealed masonry fallen from the walls and a roof supported by scaffolding in the central aisle. A shell hole had pierced the chancel. Among the visitors were Martha Nash, the

An Imber Reunion. In this picture – to the right of the aisle – can be seen members of the Dean family. Left from the aisle are Gladys Sutton (nee Dean), her grandson Andrew Johnson, Mollie Archer-Smith (nee Dean), Suzette Gordon-Johnson (nee Sutton) and Gordon Archer-Smith.

In the summer of 1961 a mobile exhibition toured the Wiltshire agricultural shows to raise the profile of the Imber campaign and to try to raise funds for the anticipated public inquiry. It included a panel painted by Kenneth Lindley with students of the Swindon School of Art with the theme 'Forever Imber', and a collection of letters from former inhabitants of the village. This picture is believed to have been taken at Melksham.

oldest surviving inhabitant at 83. Enos Matthews also attended and Nelson Carter still eager to share memories of his 32 years service with the Deans and the sheep-shearing he performed wherever it was needed. The Revd David Walser, son of the last vicar and now Vice-Principal of St Stephens Theological College, Oxford, was the guest speaker, recalling his boyhood days in the rambling vicarage. Each year there were fewer ex-residents to regale old friends with such tales. In any case, many Imberians felt with resignation that events had long passed out of their hands.

The long-awaited public inquiry was eventually set for Tuesday, 3 October and lasted two days. In a rousing article in the *Spectator*, Geoffrey Grigson had highlighted its importance. 'The temptation is to dismiss Imber as a local sentimental affair . . . But if you look first at Imber as part of Salisbury Plain, then at the Plain as part of England, you find Imber speaking for much more than its sagging doorways' The army already held one-third of the Plain and one-seventh of Wiltshire. If the army was to win, it would seal off access to some of the greatest prehistoric evidence in the British Isles and spoil the productivity of much fertile land. It deserves, he felt, to be preserved as a National Park and not 'pocked with explosions, seared with tanks and smeared with military buildings.' This could be done in less fertile areas of the North.

The Inquiry took place in the austere oak panelled council chamber of the county's headquarters at Trowbridge, its proceedings dominated by a huge map of Imber fixed to a wall. Within the packed chamber were representatives of the army and War Department who were applying for the Order, delegates of the various organisations opposing it, barristers, journalists, administrators and clerks. Among the spectators, as if reminding people what it was all about, was a scattering of former residents from Imber. Behind tables piled high with books and legal documents sat the two officials appointed by the War Works Commission to hear the evidence, Sir Harold Emmerson, the chairman, assisted by Mr Allan Lubbock who was chairman of Hampshire County Council.

In his opening remarks Sir Harold emphasised the independence of the War Works Commission which would receive the Inquiry's findings and pass on its recommendations to the Minister of Transport. Their only remit was whether or not the highways should be permanently closed and no other issues could be considered. Mr Anthony Cripps Q C, appointed by the War Office, then opened the case for closure by saying he would call four witnesses to affirm that a vital training area would be lost to the army if the roads of Imber were not stopped up. He denied that any promise had been made to Imber residents that they would be allowed to return – only that they would be given the first opportunity of re-claiming their homes – if and when the ranges were closed and the highways returned to public use. This, he said, was quite the widest undertaking of this nature ever given by the W.O. 'If Imber were restored then a further 20,000 acres would have to be compulsorily acquired, lock, stock and barrel, farms, cottages and roads. Was it right that great hardship should be inflicted on another area just to allow those who used to walk across Imber in the old days to do it again?'

St Giles Church shown through the ruins of Brown's Farm gateway.

The first witness to be called was Maj Gen C E P Harrington, until the previous day Commander of the 3rd Division and part of the U K Stategic Reserve. Following the war, he said, about ten million acres of military land

The graves of the Nash family at St Giles churchyard. To the rear is that of Evelyn Glanfield, sister of the Revd Edgar Glanfield a previous vicar of the parish.

were de-commissioned. Although it was hoped we should never be required to fight another war, it was vital to ensure that the army was properly trained if called upon. Imber was essential for that purpose. Although the main user was the School of Infantry for the use of small arms, it was also in constant use by the Strategic Reserve in conjunction with the artillery ranges at Larkhill and other land at Bulford and Tidworth. It was one of the most important areas in the U K where formation training could be carried out.

Cross-examined by Mr David Calcutt, representing the ARI, General Harrington said that Imber village was about the only built-up area in the south of England where village fighting could be taught without inconvenience to the public. He confessed, however, to Mr Kemp Homer, cross-examining for the League Against Cruel Sports, that hunting and local shoots did take place regularly across the ranges although to his knowledge no one had ever been injured. 'I think it is dangerous. I think, provided people who go on it are prepared, and know where the danger areas are, and know what to avoid riding over, you would not be risking—' At this point Mr Kemp Homer was quick to enquire whether the fox, too, received such instruction before the hunt took place!

Lt Col Carden was the Chief Instructor of the Tactical Wing of the School of Infantry at Warminster and more in touch with the day-to-day activities of the ranges. During lengthy examination he emphasised further the intensive use made of the ranges. During the past three years hundreds of units had used Imber on 1,500 occasions. The training required that men, vehicles and guns were able to deploy freely without restriction and it was therefore not possible to fence off roads or footpaths to allow public access. Neither could it be cleared thoroughly of unexploded missiles for public use especially in woodland. A recent spot check had shown as many as 60-80 high explosives along every mile of the main roads. The W D had, however, always been prepared to allow individuals with a valid reason to obtain access when the range was not in use. As regards the future use of the village the Colonel was pessimistic:

> Imber is situated on the east–west road and virtually in the centre of the area. It now consists of some 70 buildings in various stages of decay and many of them, as you saw, Sir, are little more than rubble. Of those still standing, some 26 are maintained crudely with roofing, etc., purely for training purposes. The remaining buildings are in a highly dangerous condition and likely to fall down at any time. As training in the village has in the past been conducted with live ammunition, it is dangerous, particularly to adolescents who may intrude in the ruins and the old tanks that have been used for training. It would be impracticable to clear the village of unspent missiles, even if the buildings were not dangerous.

At the end of the first day the frail figure of 84 year old Martha Nash was called to the witness box. Tearfully, she told of her interview with the War Office Land Agent in 1943. She repeated her oft-quoted assertion that he had assured her that they would return to their homes within six months. Councillor Underwood referred to the letter written by the Under-Secretary of State for War to the local M P, Sir Robert Grimston seeking compensation for Mrs Nash. In it he replied that Mr Nash was not a W D tenant as his cottage, garden and forge were within a field let to a farmer and therefore not the W D responsibility. Expenses had been paid amounting to £12 for removal to All Cannings and £5 by way of compensation for fixtures and garden produce. Subsequently Albert Nash's funeral expenses had also been paid. No compensation was due as Mrs Nash was reluctantly forced to agree.

On the second day, Mr L S Gill, the Southern Command Land Agent, was called, the first civilian witness for the W O. In his statement he said that extensive enquiries had been made to discover whether the villagers were given a promise that they could return to their homes after the war and was convinced that no such promise had been made. Councillor Underwood initiated lengthy discussion at this stage concerning a letter written by Major Whistler before his death in which he stated, 'We were not promised that we should go back but were told that the possibilities or probabilities were that we should go back in three, six or twelve months.' Mr Gill agreed this had been a probability not a promise. In any case he estimated it would take 25 men six years to clear the entire Imber area of highly dangerous ammunition.

As the Hearing progressed, much of the support that Austin had expected melted away. The Council for the Preservation of Rural England departed with hardly a whimper. The Wiltshire County Council had been placated by a promise that the status quo could be re-instated at some vague future date, the Ramblers' Association by promises of a new perimeter path. Mr Kemp Homer, counsel for the League Against Cruel Sports, at least left with a flash of defiance after his admission to being unable to refute the technical evidence of the War Office. Referring to the hunting issue he said, 'It would be a public scandal if one section of the public could use the range while the rest of Her Majesty's subjects were excluded!'

An angry exchange occurred during the evidence of the Edington vicar, Revd Ralph Dudley. Had he known of any stock belonging to perimeter farmers being injured by unexploded missiles? asked Mr Calcutt, counsel for the ARI. Mr Cripps was quickly on his feet to to cry foul. 'This was inviting hearsay,' he exclaimed. 'I had hoped not to say this', replied Mr Calcutt, 'but it is impossible to persuade a perimeter farmer to give evidence because he feels his position is prejudiced with the W D. This is a matter of grave concern.' But Mr Cripps would have none of it. They declined because they were happy with their situation, he insisted.

A further objection was made by Donald Mulcock, a senior *Salisbury Journal* reporter and member of the Wiltshire Archaeological and Natural History Society. A flagrant betrayal of trust, he said, was made by the W D in its failure to safeguard the 29 ancient monuments existing in the Imber Range area. An assurance was given by George Ratcliff, an assistant secretary at the War Office in charge of lands, that this would be looked into. It is fair to say that since that time, under the guidance of the County Archaeologist for Wiltshire, and English Heritage, more protective measures have evolved and incidents of damage have declined. The training area is now managed by the Defence Estates who employ a team of archaeologists to assist.

When Austin Underwood gave evidence, he was closely questioned on his allegiance to the CND movement, denying that he had any grudge against the army authorities. Mr Cripps probed further. 'You are a promoter of nuclear disarmament?' he asked. 'Yes I am,' replied Councillor Underwood in some exasperation at this line of questioning, 'I am also a member of the Church of England and I have stopped beating my wife!'

The Inquiry finally finished at 8.20 pm at the end of a very long second day. Mr Cripps, in his closing address, denied that the villagers were 'pushed out.' Imber was a rather tumbledown village before the evacuation; it was clearly in the last stages of decay, he said. He repeated that if the public were allowed access then the army would have to find another 20,000 acres elsewhere. Mr Calcutt (who had given his services free) felt, like Austin Underwood, that the matter had been pre-judged. Refusal to grant an adjournment had meant his case for the ARI and Amesbury District Council had been prepared very hastily. The Inquiry having been formally dismissed, everyone departed wearily for buses, cabs and the railway station to await the final decision by the Minister of Transport.

The War Office had, however, made a placatory gesture. The Imber roads were to be opened on certain occasions when the ranges were not required. Many took advantage of this when, following the Autumn exercises, the shell-pitted Gore Cross to Warminster carriageway was opened for the first time. Some even stopped to gaze at the village but, as the early winter twilight arrived, quickly moved on again. In the dying light it was no place to linger. It was still a place of ghosts, full of windowless wrecks of cottages protected by corrugated sheeting flapping eerily in the wind.

The decision of the Minister of Transport, released in early January 1962, was predictable. The army case had been a strong one and the draft order for the closure of the Imber Range roads was to stand. The Report recognised that the ranges could be restored as a farming area, that it could provide amenities for walkers, riders and motorists and that archaeological monuments existed there. However:

> Taking all these considerations into account we feel bound to come to the conclusion that they do not outweigh the manifest disadvantages which could be entailed by removal of the training range.

The ARI had gained a few concessions. The W O had agreed to a path around the perimeter of the danger area. The public was to be allowed continued access to the roads up to a maximum of 50 days.

But nothing had been said about the church; it was not in the remit of the Inquiry. In the wake of the investigation, Austin grudgingly accepted the '50 days' and fought on, continuing to pressurise the army into maintaining the church wind and weatherproof in order to keep up the profile of the village.

The ruins of Imber Court Barn, once used for Imber's village celebrations.

Imitation house blocks erected by the army and known as 'Chester Flats'.

As years passed, the press and others continued to update the story. Richard Shellabear, for example, a sixth-former at Bishop Wordsworth's School, Salisbury, had chosen Imber for his 'A' level thesis in 1976. By this time, he noted, the vicarage had completely disappeared. Of 27 buildings standing, 13 had been built by the Ministry of Defence. Only one, the Baptist Chapel, was in danger of collapse, and that subsequently disappeared. None was suitable for habitation. Imber Court had long lost its top storey and was capped by a less elegant flat concrete roof. By this time, with the uprising of terrorism in Northern Ireland, the new buildings erected by the army garishly displayed the street signs of a mock-Ulster town – Big Jim's Café, Job Centre, Angel Inn, even a police station, all diminishing the shored-up shells of earlier cottages in order to provide anti-terrorist training for Ireland and, later, other theatres of war. As the *Western Daily Press* put it in August 1978, 'Its starkly functional concrete buildings give it the ghostly air of a frontier town in the American West deserted after boom times went sour.'

A group of ex-residents at the Imber Reunion Day in September 1967. Nellie Rea and Ellen Coleman are shown talking to Martha Nash widow of the blacksmith Albert Nash.

Imber Reunion Day September 1969. Former villagers entering the normally-barricaded gateway of St Giles Church on their way to one of the annual services. They are flanked by Austin Underwood's daughters Ruth and Judith.

Leaving the church after one of the Reunion Day services at Imber in September, 1967. On the left, William Marsh greets his old friend Walter Coleman. At 88 his wife Ellen Coleman (on the right) was the oldest Imberian at the event. In the background, the Revd Ralph Dudley is shown talking to Mr G.G.L.Greenman, a committee member of the Wilts Association of Parish Councils.

One of the services held at the Imber Reunion in September 1967. Betty Hooper is seated at the extreme left of the front row.

Old friends gather outside St Giles following one of the annual services in September 1969. Left to right are: Sydney Dean (last of the village church wardens), Enos Matthews, Fanny Matthews, Nellie Rea, Percy E Plank, Walter Coleman, Walter Plank, Ellen Coleman, Mollie Archer-Smith, Fred White, Dolly White and Fred Pearce.

But attendance at the September services has remained high. Prior to these occasions, the army cleans the church, provides tables and chairs, clears the roads and cuts the grass, enabling the dwindling number of returning residents to focus their memories around St Giles. Accompanied by children, grandchildren and even some great-grandchildren, they tend their graves, meet old friends and attend the services in St Giles. For as long as it is possible they will continue, with the faithful support of a string quartet from Salisbury, to sing the evocative lines of a hymn to Peter Fletcher's tune 'Imber' with barely a trace of irony:

> *Hail blessed Giles; to whom the timid doe,*
> *Fearing the Huntsman's arrow; fled for life.*
> *Pray that we too may shelter those who fear,*
> *And bear with Christ for them the wounds of strife.*

The Revd Ralph Dudley, vicar of Edington, after the reunion services with old Imber residents. He is seen talking with Gladys Mitchell, the daughter of Albert Nash the last village blacksmith.

Epilogue

In April 1970, Betty Hooper received a letter from an Imber enthusiast, David Johnson, who for a long time had been interested in the plight of Imber village. What it said astonished her:

> Dear Betty,
>
> . . . My reason for writing is that I had the most extraordinary luck a couple of weeks ago. A former Imber resident sent me the letter his family received telling them to quit, he claims it is the only one in existence. I think he must be right...

For Cottage Tenants holding direct from W.D.

> W.D. Estate Office,
> Durrington,
> Wilts.

Dear Sir/Madam,

Imber Training Area.

Arising out of the decision that increased training facilities are to be made available in the Imber area, I regret to have to inform you that it is necessary to evacuate the major part of the Department's Imber Estate, including your dwelling.

To this end I enclose you formal notice to quit. The area has to be evacuated and available for training by *Oct 17* In this connection you will note that the formal notice to quit expires on   and it is confirmed that there will be no objection, if it assists you, to your remaining in your dwelling as tenant on sufferance until a date not later than *Dec. 17th 1943*

It is hoped that you will be able through your own efforts, to find alternative accommodation, and if appropriate, fresh employment, and that you will be able to make your own arrangements as to removal. If, however, you are in difficulty, will you please make very early contact with me at this address so that I can ensure the necessary assistance is given to you.

It is appreciated that apart from the distress the move will cause you, it must inevitably occasion direct expense for which you have no legal redress against the Department. It is however, desired to assist you in this direction as far as is practicable and equitable, and I am directed to state that the Department is prepared in principle but without prejudice to refund to you reasonable expenses incurred by you in respect of the removal of your furniture to your new home, and the travelling expenses thereto of yourself and members of your family at present living with you. In addition, if you are so unfortunate as not to be able to find alternative accommodation, and it is necessary to remove your furniture to store, the Department will refund the cost of removal to store and reasonable storage charges until you can find another house, or until the Imber area is again open for occupation, whichever is the earlier.

Further the Department is prepared if you so desire to take over from you by valuation, any produce in your garden which you are unable to harvest and take with you, and I shall be glad if you will let me have as soon as possible any claim you wish to make under this head.

> Yours faithfully,
>
> Lieut.Colonel,
> Command Land Agent,
> SOUTHERN COMMAND.

A copy of the evacuation letter sent to villagers at Imber in November, 1943.

The letter referred to was sent to the residents of Imber by Lt Col A. P. Thorne, Command Land Agent, Southern Command. Although undated, it was obviously the notice of evacuation sent to Imber villagers in November

1943. The significant words at the end of the fourth paragraph are: '. . . the Department will refund the cost of removal to store and reasonable storage charges until you can find another house, *or until the Imber area is again open for occupation, whichever is the earlier.*' This would seem to imply that, at the time, the War Office intended to return the village to civilian use after the war.

David Johnson, with two others, Richard Madigan and Rex Mutters, were very concerned over the future of the church services and the access to Imber. In 1973, they included Lt Col Thorne's letter in evidence sent to Lord Carrington, the Defence Secretary, who was conducting a review of the armed forces' land holdings with a view to finding areas that could be released. The subsequent findings of the Committee, chaired by Lord Nugent, state:

> We were sent copies of the notice of evacuation which stated that the War Department would 'refund the cost of removal to store and reasonable storage charges until you can find another house, or until the Imber area is again open for occupation, whichever is the earlier'. It was suggested to us that this letter, together with reports of what was said at the time by the officers and troops evacuating the village, are clear evidence that, despite later denials, the tenants were promised that they would be able to return to Imber...

Despite this evidence, which included a petition signed by 55 people requesting the release of Imber and the surrounding land, the Nugent Report concluded:

> We heard with sympathy about those who were residents at the time of the evacuation but we must record that the only extant document does not amount to a promise of return by any specified date; furthermore, all the evacuees were at the time tenants of the War Department and their tenancy agreements specifically reserved to the Department the right of termination.

In closing its investigation into Imber the Nugent Report recommended that the village should remain closed to the public except for relatives visiting the churchyard and that the ecclesiastical authorities should even be invited to consider whether the annual services should be continued.

In 1991, Mr Heseltine, the Environment Secretary, approved a recommendation from the Boundaries Commission that the parish of Imber should be abolished. With its passing the veteran campaigners were forced to concede that their campaign was almost over. Even Betty Hooper, whose life-long research into the Imber story has greatly assisted this book, was forced to exclaim, 'I'm afraid it is all a dead dodo now'.

After suffering from Parkinson's Disease for fifteen years, Austin Underwood died on Easter Day, 11 April 1993, after a fall, only months before the fiftieth anniversary of the evacuation, which was celebrated at the Imber services by one of the largest gatherings ever. With his passing, the ARI dwindled away. Betty Hooper died in December 1999. The new millennium sees a faithful congregation of Imber friends and relations of the second and third generation still continuing to return, to tend the graves and attend the services in a church that is growing more frail with the passing years. When that is forced to close, people will be left entirely with their memories.

An Imber Reunion in the early 1990s. Austin Underwood is shown talking to women from Greenham Common shortly before his death. Margaretta d'Arcy is holding the video camera.

Bibliography

Note: PRO = Public Record Office, Kew; *SJ* = *Salisbury & Winchester Journal*; *WANHM* = *Wiltshire Archaeological & Natural History Magazine*; WRO = Wiltshire & Swindon Record Office, Trowbridge.

Chapter 1

Victoria history of Wiltshire, vols 2, 1955; 8, 1965

Hoare, Sir Richard Colt, *Ancient Wiltshire*, vol 1, 1812

Hoare, Sir Richard Colt, *Modern Wiltshire: Heytesbury Hundred*, 1822

Grinsell, L V, *The archaeology of Wessex*, 1958

Noyes, Ella, *Salisbury Plain*, 1913

Whitlock, Ralph, *Salisbury Plain*, 1955

WANHM, vols 39, 500; 40, 362; 41, 212; 47, 81-4

Revels, G S, *A thousand years of history: a short guide to St Giles church and the parish of Imber, Wilts*, [c. 1970]

Speed, John, *Map of Wiltshire*, 1611

Watkin, Bruce, *Imber*, 1984

Barnes, Ian, pers. comm. 29 Mar 2001

Hooper, Betty, private papers

Morrison, Jean, private papers

SJ, 1 Nov 1773

Devizes & Wiltshire Gazette, 23 Jan 1840

Chapter 2

WRO census returns, 1841-91

Post Office Directory, 1859

Noyes, *op. cit.*

Hudson, W H, *A shepherd's life*, 1910

Hooper, Betty, private papers

Morrison, Jean, private papers

Shellabear, Richard, unpublished thesis, 1976

Bristol Journal, 30 Jun 1843

SJ, 11 Feb 1793

Chapter 3

WRO census returns 1841-91

WRO 1026/19: Imber churchwardens' accounts, 1743-1923

WRO T/A Imber, tithe map and apportionment, 1838

Kelly's directories of Wiltshire, various issues 1891-1939

Warburton, William, *An account, with map, of all schools. . . in Wilts*, 1859

Revels, *op. cit.*

Hooper, Betty, private papers, and interview, Feb 1997

Archer-Smith, Molly, interview, 15 Mar 2000

Watkin, *op. cit.*

SJ, 27 Sep 1841

Chapter 4

WRO 1026/19

WANHM, vol. 42, 73-5

Kelly op. cit.

James, N D G, *Plain soldiering*, 1987

Reeves, Marjorie, *Sheep bell and ploughshare*, 1978

Wheatley, Dennis, *The time has come: memoirs: officer and temporary gentleman*, 1978

McEvoy, Patrick, *The gorse and the briar*, 1938

Revels, *op. cit.*

Murray, Venetia (ed.), *Where have all the cowslips gone? Wessex memories*, 1985

Tennant, Pamela, *Village notes, and some other papers*, 1900

Hooper, Betty, private papers [reminiscences of Gladys Dean, and diary of Thomas Stone, 1895]

Morrison, Jean, private papers [reminiscences of Percy Pye]

Crawford, T S, *Wiltshire and the great war*, 1999

Wiltshire Family History Society Journal, Aug 1988; Jan 1989

Wiltshire Life, Dec 1997

Shellabear, Richard, *op. cit.*

Mitchell, Derrick, interview 24 Sep 2000

Marshall, David, pers. comm. Nov 2000

Yeates, Jack, interview 25 Apr 2000

Gentry, Gwen, interview and pers. comm. 2000

Hooper, Betty, private papers (reminiscences of Revd Frank Maidment]

This England, winter 1980

Country Life, Sep 1998

Wiltshire Gazette, 29 Dec 1921; 30 Mar 1961

SJ, 29 Nov 1957; 6 Dec 1957

Wiltshire Times, 3 Feb 1961

Warminster Journal, 5 May 1967

Chapter 5

PRO WO32/21804
Mee, Arthur, *Wiltshire: cradle of our civilisation*, 1939
Hutchings, Monica, *The special smile*, 1951
Hooper, Betty, private papers
Mitchell, Derrick, interview 24 Sep 2000
Meaden, Reg, pers. comm. Mar 2000
Whitlock, Ralph, *op. cit.*
Bateman, Denis C, 'Incident at Imber', *After the battle*, 49, 1985, 16-25
Olivier, Edith, *Wiltshire*, 1951
Wiltshire Family History Society Journal, Aug 1988; Jan 1989
Watkin, Bruce, *op. cit.*
Saga Magazine, 1996
James, N D G, *op. cit.*
Archer-Smith, Mollie, interview 15 Mar 2000
Streeting, Audrey. interview 27 Apr 2000
Hooper, Betty, interview Feb 1997
Gilbert, Martin, *The day the war ended*, 1995
Revels, G S, *op. cit.*
Shellabear, Richard, *op. cit.*
The Times, 14-17 Apr 1942; 5 Apr 1948

News Chronicle, 11 Nov 1943
Wiltshire Gazette & Herald, 28 Jun 1984
SJ, 28 Nov 1957; 10 Sep 1987; 23 Mar 1989; 17-31 Aug 1989

Chapter 6

James, N D G, *op. cit.*
Street, Pamela, *Portrait of Wiltshire*, 1971
Hutchings, Monica, *op. cit.*
Whitlock, Ralph, *op. cit.*
Hooper, Betty, interview Feb 1997
Archer-Smith, Mollie, interview 15 Mar 2000
Crawford, Terry, pers. comm. 2000-1
WANHM, vols. 51, 227-8; 52, 268
Wiltshire Family History Society Journal, Jan 1989
Barr, Jenny, 'The mourning of Imber', *News Focus*, 1993
Saga Magazine, 1996
Gentry, Gwen, interview 2000
contemporary local and national newspapers

Chapter 7

PRO WO 32/21804; WO 32/17498

contemporary local and national newspapers
Punch, Jan 1961
Weekly Post, 11 Feb 1961
Wiltshire Family History Society Journal, Jan 1989
Crawford, T S, *op. cit.*
Underwood, Mary, pers. comm. 2000-1

Chapter 8

Proceedings of Public Inquiry, County Hall, Trowbridge, 3-4 Oct 1961
WRO 2860/1-10: papers of Austin Underwood
contemporary local and national newspapers
Annetts, Sophie, interview Mar 2001, pers. comm. 2000

Epilogue

Nugent, George (Baron), *Report of the Defence Lands Committee*, 1973
Hooper, Betty, interview Feb 1997
Thorne, Lt Col A P, letter to villagers, Nov 1943
Underwood, Mary, pers. comm. 2000-1

Picture Credits

The author would like to acknowledge the following for permission to use illustrations. If anyone has an earlier claim, the matter will be put right in any subsequent editions:

Stephen Moody, the sketch maps on pages iv and 22
Wiltshire Archaeological and Natural History Society Library, Devizes, the John Buckler painting, page 5
Rosalind Hooper, pages 10, 14, 17, 18, 19, 20, 25, 26, 29, 30 (top), 31, 32, 34, 35, 36, 37, 38, 39, 41, 42, 43, 47, 48, 49 (bottom), 53, 54, 56, 57, 58, 61, 62, 66, 67, 71, 73, 74, 76, 77, 78 80, 86, 88, 89, 90, 91, 97, 152

John Rebbeck, page 6
Salisbury Museum, pages 21 and 45
Mollie Archer-Smith, pages 24, 27, 79, 82, 102, 107
Gwen Gentry, pages 28, 30 (bottom), 64, 65, 114
Suzette Gordon-Johnson, pages 40, 49 (top), 50, 5l, 52, 69, 75, 113
Jack Yeates, page 60
Audrey Streeting, pages 72, 85, 99
Gladys Mitchell, page 83

Mary Underwood, pages 111, 118, 123, 126, 127, 134, 135, 138, 140, 141, 143, 144, 145, 147, 148, 154, 155, 156, 157, 160
Salisbury Journal, pages 124 and 140
Bath and Wiltshire Chronicle and Herald, page 132
Richard Shellabear, page 153
Southern Evening Echo, page 154 (bottom)

Index

Note: references in **bold** type are to illustrations.

Lightning Source UK Ltd.
Milton Keynes UK
UKOW01f2318150217
294529UK00001B/76/P